Brown Feathers

Brown Feathers

Waterfowling Tales and
Upland Dreams

Steven J. Mulak

Stackpole Books

Published by
STACKPOLE BOOKS
Cameron and Kelker Streets
P.O. Box 1831
Harrisburg, PA 17105

Printed in the United States of America

10 9 8 7 6 5 4 3 2 1

Library of Congress Cataloging-in-Publication Data
Mulak, Steven J.
  Brown feathers.

  I. Title.
PS3563.U387B7   1987   813'.54   87-7120
ISBN 0-8117-0255-3

For Mark Dilts, my mentor

Contents

Foreword

STEVE MULAK and I first crossed paths in 1981. His manuscript, "Wax and Wane," had just arrived in the mail and was another unsolicited article sitting on my desk, waiting its turn to be read. Nothing special at first, no outward clues as to what it contained. But when I finally read it, and came to understand what duck hunting meant to its author, I knew right there that *Sports Afield* had found another contributor.

As it turns out, we had to send "Wax" back for a little cutting. As an editor, I'm always curious about what's going to happen when I send a manuscript back to an author for a revise. Some authors get offended and don't even respond to your request; some give it a try and return something that's worse than the original; and some, the minority, send you back exactly what you are hoping for. They understand that you're trying to help them out, that they're not beyond improvement.

Steve proved himself to be in that latter category. His revised "Wax" came back finely tuned and shorter, but still lively, still insightful. Rather than recoiling at suggestions for improvement, Steve responded with unbridled enthusiasm. It showed . . . and it always does with Steve.

From that point on, we've had as good an editor-writer relationship as I imagine you could have. We'll get on the phone and kick ideas around . . . discuss stories . . . discuss the magazine . . . discuss writing . . . even discuss the fact that we really ought to go hunting together one of these days. We will, too. I know that, because Steve wants to do it. And, as I've found out over the years, when Steve sets his mind to something, he doesn't give up until the job is done. And that can mean coaxing a friend to go woodcock hunting with him; or coming up with a good story idea and following it through until the manuscript is in the mail; or busting into an impossible alder tangle because there just *has* to be a bird in there somewhere!

In this book, you're going to find a number of different stories. Some will make you laugh; others will surprise you with their observations and insights; some will make you reminisce of days gone by; some will make you itch for tomorrow.

Of one thing I'm sure: In this book, you will be reading the work of a man whose love of hunting and of writing is insurpassable. His enthusiasm is infectious, and the more you read of this book, the more you'll feel that something inside of you is beginning to flare up too. In fact, by the time you put this book down, I'll bet that you'll be thinking of oiling up the old 20-gauge again.

Jay Cassell

Epigraph

"The best thing about hunting and fishing," the Old Man said, "is that you don't have to actually do it to enjoy it. You can go to bed every night thinking of how much fun you had twenty years ago, and it all comes back as clear as moonlight."

—Robert Ruark, *The Old Man's Boy Grows Older*

First Snow

There have always been two major problems, man and man, and man and earth, his environment. Neither stand alone, and the false solutions always turn out to be the ones that ignore that eternal kinship.

—Hal Borland, *Sundial of the Seasons*

THE BLUE-SHADOWED IMPRINT of the truck tires in the new snow is so exact that it seems to ache. The parallel tracks branch away from the few others on the road, almost like a railroad spur that the truck has ridden to the end of rather than created. I stand for a moment, leaning on the open door, watching the vapor clouds of my breath dissipate in the morning air. The next few hours that I'll spend here loom up before me: When I return, will I be elated, or will I be disappointed with the way I've hunted? What memories will I make here this morning? I uncase the gun, then feel through the outsides of my pockets for the things I know are there—ammunition, knife, keys, wallet.

Hazel sits on the floor of the truck, her furiously wagging tail belying her patient demeanor. There is no doubt in my mind that she uses as much energy waiting to hunt as she does at full throttle. I glance up and down the road, then bring her out with a quiet "heel." We cross to the edge of the valley, then when I've eased my way down the short bank, I whistle her on. She races past me, kicking up a roostertail of snow. I slip a pair of shells into the barrels and start off, angling toward the brook. Mister Kulig's covert is an old friend that knew me when I was training my first bird dog. We'll hunt in a circuit that follows one of the big stream's feeder brooklets up into the hills beyond Mister Kulig's farm, then follow another brook back down again.

My ears are assaulted by the quiet. The powdery snow acts as a sound absorber, and the effect is eerily like being in a small room. Even Hazel's bell is quiet. She crosses my path thirty yards in front of me as she works the cover.

THE SNOW had fallen between midnight and dawn. Even though the past week had been consistently cold, I was surprised to see snow this early. I was a bit jaded toward New England weather after a series of mild winters, but the calendar reminded me that there was nothing early about a mid-November snowfall.

I was mixing pancake batter when my daughters came downstairs. "Hey Dad! Did you see? It snowed out!"

"*What!* You're kidding! Holy smokes, look at that! I didn't even notice!" My humor played to appreciative giggles.

"Can we go skiing at the golf course?"

"The radio says that the schools aren't closed . . ." (frowns) ". . . and there's really not enough snow to ski on . . ." (deeper frowns) ". . . and it'll probably all be melted by lunchtime, anyway" (utter gloom).

As she combed the youngest's hair, my wife offered, "You girls don't seriously think your father would take a day off from hunting, do you?"

I spooned the first pancakes onto the grill before addressing the gloom. "I'll tell you what—if there's still snow on the ground this afternoon, I'll have the skis on the car when you guys get home, and all you'll have to do is jump into your knickers and we'll all be skiing in five minutes. Okay?"

"Okay." The gloom lifted only slightly.

A flock of evening grosbeaks chose that moment to make their first appearance of the season at the window feeder, and the subject of skiing was suspended as we crowded for a close-up look at the strange and colorful birds.

I STEP ACROSS a low stone wall where only the leafless stems of poison ivy break the surface of the snow. Winter is a simple, uncomplicated season. The windless snowfall has left an inch-high ridge on every exposed twig and blade of grass, and the white expanse of the forest floor is filigreed with blue shadows in the slanting morning sunlight. A rabbit bounces away at the head of a lengthening series of tracks on the unblemished surface. As through a liquid, tiny shock waves radiate out through the snow at each of his bounds.

I should have spray-painted the dog day-glo orange. In the white landscape, my nearly all-white setter is a fast-moving shadow that my eyes refuse to remain focused upon. If the snow were wet, her bell would clog and I'd really have a problem keeping track of her. She checks back after each cast, but in her third season she has finally begun to suspect that I cannot scent birds after all, and she's grown more independent. Rightly so: In her three autumns, her nose has processed more grouse data than I've gathered in a lifetime of hunting.

We follow the stream to the confluence of two brooklets. My ears track Hazel's progress as she skirts the far side of a row of hemlocks.

She pops into view immediately in front of me, and my eyes are on her when she skids to an unsure halt just beyond the last evergreen. Her sidelong look is not so much a point as a questioning *"What the hell . . .?"* There is a flurry of movement under the hemlock, then a gray flash on the far side. Muffled by the snow, the grouse's flush is strangely quiet. No shot is possible. Hazel, with a different perspective than I, stands watching the bird's flight. As I start forward, a second bird flushes from the same tree, this one more clearly seen than the first. His retreat hugs the far side of the hemlock row. I swing ahead of the bird and fire, but then glimpse him passing beyond the trees ten yards farther on. Shooting through screening branches is standard procedure in grouse shooting, but today the snow-laden boughs effectively absorb my shot pellets. I would have thought I had him.

From the far side of the hemlocks, I make an educated guess as to where the birds have flown: The valley is fairly open, so they would have flown long and most likely have crossed all the way to the thick stuff on the far side. My setter is casting back and forth, searching the snow for a downed bird. "Thanks for the vote of confidence, Hazel, but he kept going." I start off, but she continues her search, and it isn't until the third time that I whistle to her that she joins me. All the commands I've taught her are positive, and I have no way of telling her "Whoops, I missed."

When last I hunted this valley, the trees seemed aflame. Today the only color is an occasional sprig of princess pine that peeks through the snow, and in the ruddy bark of the chokecherries. December is coming: The color is gone, and the grouse have grown wilder and smarter. Most are birds-of-the-year that have never known the defoliated world of late autumn, which explains why the weeks immediately after the leaves are down are the grouse hunter's favorite time of the year. But the birds soon learn what they must if they are to survive in a leafless woodland, and by early winter the hunter finds that a box of shells lasts a lot longer than it did just a few weeks before.

Hemlocks are a favorite winter retreat for grouse. My guess that the birds flew here is confirmed almost as soon as we enter the stand on the far side of the valley—twenty yards in, I feel as much as hear an overhead grouse flush, close by but unseen. There is no telling his direction, so we push on in the hopes for a chance at the second bird. From the thick evergreens there is a continuous cascade of snow created by my passing. I brush the accumulations from the gun barrels, thinking I've found yet another reason to shoot with both eyes open.

We work the rest of the length of the brook course without moving another bird, and emerge below the little dam that forms Mister Kulig's pond. There are often grouse in the swampy area along the outlet, but Hazel reports that they are feeding elsewhere this morning.

Laurel has taken over the timbered hillside along the pond's edge. As usual, the brakes are littered with deer sign, but today there is a profusion of grouse tracks mixed among the cloven deer prints. Below me, at the very edge of the frozen pond, the dog's bell goes silent in a laurel thicket. A grouse flushes far ahead of her point as soon as I start downhill, and he sails two hundred yards just above the snow-covered ice, paired with his blue shadow immediately below. From my elevated vantage point, I am able to watch the bird climb over the treetops on the far shore, then fly another two hundred yards before dropping down into the woods. Grouse, of course, *never* fly more than a hundred and fifty yards when flushed. I wrote that in an article once.

Later, I sit with Hazel at the far end of the covert, feeding her dog biscuits as I pull the ice balls from between her pads. Although we hunted the laurel thoroughly, the far-flying grouse must have been the last of a group that departed before we arrived. Or else he had spent a very busy morning making footprints all by himself. On the return we'll cross Sam's swamp, named for a friend from Texas who traveled two thousand miles to shoot a grouse, then blew the only good chance he had in a week of hunting. We'll work the other shore of the pond, then follow another brook course down into the valley. When the dog biscuits are all gone, Hazel is eager to go, but I sit a while longer and watch the flock of waxwings that seems intent on gleaning every last berry from the shrubs around the deadfall where I sit.

Hunting again, I hear a flock of crows beyond the next hill. I stuff my orange hat into my gamebag, whistle in the dog, and hide on the shadowed side of an old oak tree. The first series of long *"crawww's"* I play on the wooden call only serves to silence the flock, but the initial squawk of the next set brings a raucous chorus of answers. Hazel's tail begins to fan the snow as she sits at my feet, watching the treetops. Although I like to think I know just when to shut up, I almost always call too much, so when the first of the oncoming flock appears, I let the call dangle on its lanyard. They circle widely without dropping altitude, asking crow questions that I itch to answer.

After waiting a very long minute, I have the call at my lips when a crow silently passes overhead from behind me, barely fifty feet up. I scramble to rush a pair of shots, both of which pass behind the bird.

The calls of the flock change to short warning cries that fade into the distance. I tuck the call back inside my shirt, put the empties into my pocket, and smile an "Aw-shit" grin to myself. I like crows. They're handsome birds in their own way, and I admire their ability to survive by cooperation in a winter world most other species choose to abandon. But mostly they're fun: In a contest of wits, I seldom win out.

If the day has warmed up, I haven't noticed it. The sun is coldly bright as it climbs slightly higher along its shallow winter arc. A wisp of breeze begins blowing snow off the trees, and the effect is lovely. The Finns, I think it is, have no single word in their language for the general term snow. Instead, living as they do in a world of sleighs and skis, they have a multitude of nouns for the various types and conditions of snow. Today's powdery stuff is certainly a far cry from the heavy wet snow associated with suburban driveways and coronaries. When last we hunted this stretch, Hazel pointed a half-dozen woodcock. What most stands out in my memory is that I had seen one bird on the ground ten feet in front of the dog's point, obvious because its normally perfect camouflage was too dark for the pale beech leaves matted on the ground. The woods—or perhaps it's just my expectations—are different now that the woodcock are gone. Not worse, and certainly not better. Just different.

I look up, at the sound of a grouse flush. The bird breaks from the pines twenty yards ahead of me, already in full flight, passing to the rear beyond my right shoulder. I see him clearly, but my fastest response can't catch up with the bird and my shot passes behind him. He dips and curves left and is gone. The moment is quickly over. As I stand staring at the spot where he disappeared, a hemlock bough releases its weight of snow and springs upward, almost like an "amen" to the event. I had grinned at my muffed shot at the crow, but this one leaves me tight-lipped. Shots like that are a challenge to my abilities, and too frequently I miss. I have no excuse—I'm simply not good enough to make fast cross shots with consistency.

The dog checks back, and I whistle her in. For a moment I stand with the gun open and see again the bird hurtling through the dappled sunlight in the clearing, and once more feel the twinge of panic at not being able to catch up with him. What was spectacular was not the shot but the chance. And afterward what is full is not my gamebag, but my memory. I drop a fresh shell into the barrel and wave Hazel ahead. My grimace fades into a smile, more of appreciation than amusement.

We pursue the grouse to the far side of the ridge. There is an open field below, so he must have flown into the scrub on the near hillside.

I tell myself that I am sure the bird is here. When we've hunted farther along the ridge than I estimate he flew, we loop downward and work back closer to the edge of the field. We've already covered a lot of places where he's not, so each step brings us closer to the moment we'll find him. Some folks call that sort of thing faith. I like to think of it as a combination of applied experience and positive thinking.

Ahead of me the dog's bell goes silent. I move up but can't see her in the brushy pines and oaks. I wait, gun at ready. Nothing. I move forward another cautious fifteen feet but still cannot see her point. I whistle to her softly, and she replies by allowing her bell a single ". . . *ding* . . ." Ah, she's in the heavy stuff at the edge of the field, directly in front of me. I move toward the sound of her bell, and then hear the grouse flush. The gun comes up, but I have no target. The first I see of the bird is as he enters the trees fifty yards away. The grouse we moved at the pond edge was the exception: Grouse don't normally cross open spaces unless they're pushed. This one has skirted the edge of the low cover rather than cross the open field.

Hazel comes in. In her eyes is the wild look that says she's been "in birds." I scratch her ears in reward for her productive but unseen point.

We hunt our way back along the little valley, and recross the stream where the two feeder brooks join. At the wall I find my own bootprints, still looking as fresh as when I made them. A squirrel has left his tracks along the stones, and there are several tiny prints made by songbirds. And here, just beyond the shadow cast by the old wall, a line of grouse tracks crosses over my own. I had been entertaining thoughts of the lunch that waits back at the truck, but suddenly all that seems far away. Daniel Boone, tracker of the untamed wilderness, crouches low to examine the animal spoor. All that the tracks in the snow tell me is that a grouse walked along the wall heading that-a-way, and since they pass over my own, it was sometime after I passed here four hours ago. Tracks are fun to look at, but I've never had much luck following them. I'm hardly good enough to tell the age of a print in terms of hours, and more often than not they only confuse me, as a feeding bird crosses and recrosses its own path. I'm better off putting my trust in Hazel's nose.

Paralleling the brook and the old wall, we start off. Lunch can wait. My positive thinking goes to work again: The grouse was strolling down to the overgrown orchard I remember at the bottom of the valley for a snack. There's plenty of cover and food among the junipers and bittersweet that have taken over the place, and he's probably feeding there right now. My setter casts through the cover as she should, but I find that I keep stretching my neck to be sure the grouse tracks are still following the wall, just as someone might peek at the covered cards in a game of solitaire. I whistle to Hazel and curve up onto the sidehill, mostly to take my eyes off the trail of grouse prints. A hundred yards farther along, we slant down into the overgrown apple trees.

Hunting through the orchard, we reach the wall. The snow where the grouse's trail should be is undisturbed. I whistle to the dog and turn to the left, back up the valley, and find that my grip on my gunstock has unconsciously tightened in expectation. Hazel's cast takes her as far as the edge of the brook. As she turns and starts back, she stops abruptly in midstride, head and tail high and her eyes bulging in a look that announces, "Your bird is *right here!*" Under the juniper, the grouse realizes he is trapped and takes wing before I've advanced three steps in his direction. He comes out in an explosion of snow, heading across the brook. My shot catches him as he passes behind a small pine sapling, and he tumbles in a second shower of snow. The distance can't be more than twenty-five yards, but the stream runs between Hazel and the bird. She tiptoes across the shelf ice with only one hind foot breaking through, then runs to make the retrieve. The trackless snow is littered with bits of gray fluff. Every other hit must draw a like amount of feathers, but they normally go unnoticed in the fallen leaves on the forest floor. Hazel brings the steel-gray bird to me and I know the day is complete.

I'M NOT SO OLD or so long out of school that I don't recall the theme papers we were required to write; "How I Spent My Summer Vacation," or "What Thanksgiving Means to Me." Today's composition, class, will be entitled "What Hunting Season Means to Me." In a storybook setting like this, chewing a sweet birch twig as I follow a bird dog back to the truck, that one is easy, ma'am. Grown men spend too much of their lives in a world of asphalt and concrete, or in my own case, in the engine room of a steel ship where the only contact with nature is the marine growth that fouls the strainers. When even the decorative plants are plastic, it's tough to see yourself as one of Nature's children. But here, with wisps of wind strewing diamonds into the sunbeams and the not-unpleasant sting of snowflakes against my face, I can believe again that the weight in my gamebag is more important than any other kind of success that life has to offer. What does the hunting season mean to me? I *live* for it. I recall hearing a famous circus aerialist state that life for him was a series of waits between performances. At the time, I thought to myself, "How shallow." Yet, I find I've begun to think of my own life in terms of autumns and the months spent waiting for the next one. Others may think of that as being superficial, but I know better.

I let Hazel into the truck, and brush the windstrewn snow from the windshield. Next to the driver's door are the footprints I made several hours before. I think back to my pondering thoughts at the time, and reflect that among the items I am returning with is a full limit of memories. That the snow may soon melt or refreeze into something less lovely than it has been this morning only makes my limit all the more precious. Hazel peers out the window at me. Her tail clearly says that she is eager to be on our way to the next covert. I smile to myself. Tomorrow is yet another fraction of a season that is divided among all too few days, but right now I've got just about an hour to return home and break out the skis from storage and get the carrier rack onto the car.

Housman's Dog

The time you won your town the race
We chaired you through the market place:
Man and boy stood cheering by
And home we brought you, shoulder high.

WITH THE DRAKE wood duck in his mouth, Woodie emerged from the flooded rushes across from us and stood belly-deep in the water, looking for my brother. John got to his feet, rocking the boat a bit, and waved his hat in the air as he called to his dog. The pup started toward us and seemed surprised when he fell off the submerged river bank into deep water, but he came up swimming. With the duck in his mouth, his breath came as a series of audible wheezes as he dog-paddled back. The silence that a midmorning drizzle brings to a November marsh made the pup's breathing sound all the more labored. Several of the decoys in the rig turned and followed in the dog's wake as he swam through the spread, and the combined effect of the dragging anchors all but stopped his progress. John was quickly there at the edge of the bank, encouraging his dog.

"C'mon, ol' Woodie . . . C'mon, boy . . ."

The pup seemed in trouble, and I began to pull the boat out of its hiding place. John waved me back. The dog struggled to inch closer to shore, and after a moment John was able to reach out and grab the dog's chain collar to haul him in. Woodie laid the duck in the shallow water at my brother's feet, then backed up in expectation of another round of the familiar "go-fetch" game of his training sessions.

"Hey, this is Steven's. Go take it to him." John held out the bird, but Woodie wanted it thrown. I clapped John on the back and shook his hand.

"Congratulations! That's terrific. I'm glad I was a part of it." This was the pup's first retrieve under the gun, and the three of us stood around grinning at each other over it all.

We tossed the retrieved decoys back into the rig. Until the end of his short life, Woodie would never figure out the mystery of the underwater decoy cords, and he rearranged our spreads on his every retrieve.

Beyond the boat, out in the swirl of the current, I noticed the visual echo that was my empty shell. It bobbed in the eddy, almost but not quite shipping water each time it yawed. As I stared at the empty, my thoughts drifted to John and his puppy-become-retriever: My brother had long held the conviction that he just did not have the spare time necessary to train and keep a hunting dog of his own, and had resigned himself to the role of a hunter who enjoys only other people's dogs. But one day a two-week-old golden retriever puppy was suddenly thrust upon him—its mother had been killed by a car, and wouldn't he please take one of the pups?

Woodie was bottle-fed through his infancy and named for the ducks on the new waterfowling stamp, and here, six months and dozens of training sessions later, had just made a retriever man out of my brother. I smiled at the thought and glanced to where Woodie shared the stern seat with John. They hunkered low together, and it took me a moment to realize that the moving reflections on the water belonged to a pair of mallards they had spotted winging into the rig . . .

> Today, the road all runners come,
> Shoulder high we bring you home
> And set you at your threshold down:
> Townsman of a stiller town.

THE REFLECTIONS in the dark water matched a pair of flaring whistlers in the snowy sky. My opportunity for a shot was lost in a daydream, but John's gun said that he had been paying attention. One of the pair continued on a down-sloping tangent to the upward curve of his partner's flight, and hit the river out beyond the shelf ice midriver.

Woodie stood on the boat seat, intently watching the bird's descent. Now in his third season, he had at last come around to agreeing with John's insistence that he stay put and mark the bird's fall.

"Go ahead . . . Go get 'em, Woodie." The dog turned a circle on the boat seat, then with just a suggestion of a push from my brother, jumped into the water. Once out, he swam strongly, catching only one of the decoys as he passed through the rig. He reached the ice and climbed out, searching the water beyond. The whistler must have made a move that was seen only by the dog, for he suddenly sprinted forward and plunged into the open water.

"Look at that!" John grinned. He was on his feet, with both hands shading his eyes as he stared out through the snow. The dog was in the water, swimming with a renewed purpose. The bird surfaced momentarily, then dived again. He was a hundred yards from us.

Then, abruptly, the action seemed to stop. The shelves of ice had been drifting along imperceptibly with the river's slow current, but now one had struck something that caused it to stop. The sheet nearer to us pivoted on the hung-up floe, and the open water beyond began to shrink as the distance closed. Woodie was still swimming, waiting for the duck to surface again.

"Woodie! *Woodie!*" John waved his arms over his head, but the dog would not look back. "Oh shit." He was suddenly very ashen. The sheet of ice continued on its collision course, and the danger to the dog became increasingly evident.

I sat riveted to the seat. With fifty yards of moving river ice between our boat and Woodie, there seemed little we could do. But John was in the shallow water, pulling on the bow line. "C'mon. Let's get out there."

I got out and pushed at the transom. "John, what can we possibly do?"

He spoke to me, but his eyes were on the shrinking patch of water beyond the ice. "This ain't no story in some friggin' hunting magazine, for Chrissakes . . . That's *my dog* out there . . ." He left the rest unsaid. I started the motor.

When I looked up, Woodie was swimming for the edge and appeared about to save himself from the crush. Then the whistler surfaced again, saw the dog, and turned and swam away. Woodie followed.

"*Woodie!*" John yelled frantically, then lifted his gun and fired two shots over his head. Unheeding, the dog closed the gap on the swimming duck, but then the whistler dived again. There was only ten yards of open water left, and that was closing fast. I added my shouts to John's.

Just before the floes sheared together, the dog attempted to climb out, but the current beneath the moving ice pulled him under, and in a moment there was no open water to be seen.

John turned to me in panic. "Quick—give me your flotation jacket."

"No." I was sure of my answer. Instead, I handed him an oar. "Here—use this. We'll break our way to him."

We hit the shelf ice with the motor at full throttle. Both of us were knocked off our seats, but the impact opened a long series of cracks. Things immediately began to move downriver again: We had inadvertently freed the hung-up floe. Standing, we rocked the boat from side to side and made surprisingly good progress through the rotted ice. Using the oars to push the broken ice out of the way, we both worked frantically—until the omen appeared: The whistler floated out from under the ice, belly-up.

This time, it was me who cursed.

We continued to break ice, but the urgency had gone out of our search.

I didn't notice the dog until we were just a few feet from him. He was completely submerged, and seemed an incongruous patch of tan in the dark water. I stopped the motor and started forward to help, but John waved me back. He reached out and grabbed the dog's chain collar and hauled him in. The legs were already stiff. We were a half-mile downriver from our decoys. I started the motor and swung the boat around.

John turned away and pretended to watch the shoreline slip by. His face showed no emotion. Thankfully, conversation was all but impossible over the drone of the motor. My gaze continued to drift to the lifeless form in the bow. Woodie was dead. Ice formed on his fur. I recalled his occasional taste for a badly shot up duck, and how his whole body would wag when he was happy. He had been a one-man dog in every sense of the word, and John held up his part of the bargain by being blind to Woodie's every fault. With tears freezing on my cheeks, I reflected on how right John had been: This wasn't no story in some friggin' hunting magazine, with a miraculous retrieve and a happy ending. The duck stamp under the plastic cover on our licenses showed a pair of Canadas feeding peacefully, but waterfowling is a game with death for the loser—and it isn't always the ducks who lose. Any hunter who goes out onto a tide-swept marsh or a frozen river without the realization of all the implications of that fact is a fool.

Overhead, motion caused me to glance skyward. A single drake whistler sailed out of the snow, his wings set on our decoy spread up ahead . . .

> Smart lad, to slip betimes away
> From fields where glory does not stay.
> And early though the laurel grows,
> It withers quicker than the rose.

I GLANCED UP at the overhead motion. A single teal sailed out of the October blue sky, his wings set on our decoys. He swung by with a blurring speed, and the lead I gave him might be measured in boxcar lengths. When the shot caught him, the illusion was that of a sprinter tripping: The teal was in graceful flight one moment, and the next was cartwheeling through the air with his wings, feet, and head forming a fivepointed star. He actually bounced when he hit the water, but promptly righted himself and began swimming away.

Next to me, Bingo was a cocked pistol on the boat seat. John said, "Go fetch"; and it seemed the dog might jump all the way to the crippled bird. He swam powerfully. At his approach the duck dived. The dog trod water, his upper body above the surface, waiting. When the teal showed himself again ten yards away, Bingo lunged at him, nearly running out of the water in his scramble to get to the bird. The teal dived again, but so did the dog, and when he came up a moment later, he had the duck in his mouth.

To his credit, my brother didn't pretend that Woodie's death in the ice had never happened or that it was somebody else's fault. That he continued to hunt as before and started another golden retriever almost immediately was the mark of the man's character. But there can only be one "first" dog in anyone's life, and John felt that he had been cheated out of his. The unfulfilled promise of what Woodie might have become haunted our every outing. That this new golden had far more natural ability mattered little to John, if he even realized it at all. Indicative of his indifference was the fact that his children had named Bingo, and after three years John referred to him only as "the dog."

There was nothing labored about Bingo. He was a massively built golden, and whatever he did seemed to come easily to him. He needed no help getting into the boat, nearly vaulting from the water to the seat. He sat there with the live teal in his mouth, both of them blinking at me. The full-plumage drake looked for all the world like he had just flown off the duck stamp. After I dispatched the bird and Bingo shook the water out of his coat, I placed an arm around his neck and playfully grabbed his muzzle. "Mister Bingo Barnes, sir, you are one mighty fine bird dog."

Bingo grinned his open-mouthed dog's grin back at me.

At the other end of the boat, John took no notice of our antics. He stared out onto the early autumn marsh. I tried to follow his gaze, but it went much farther than I could see, past the decoys and the distant shore, beyond the horizon to a snowy river where ice floes sheared together and whistlers flew low across the dark water.

> Now you will not swell the rout
> Of lads that wore their honours out:
> Runners whom renown outran
> And the name died before the man.

Wax and Wane

At times the waterfowl season seems shorter than its allotted number of days . . . times when an entire season can be compressed into a single day on the marshes:

5:40 A.M. The silence is overpowering. Nearly straight overhead Andromeda and Pegasus shine boldly in the October sky, and although the first hint of dawn shows in the east, the starlight is still reflected brightly in the water. I continually glance upward in amazement. Crystal-clear dawns are not normally associated with promising waterfowling . . . except today. This morning we'll have fine shooting at unwary natives, and weather won't be a factor. It's opening day, and the hunting won't be as fruitful until a month from now when the first winter storms begin pushing the migrants down from the Maritimes.

I finish securing the boat, then pull the overhanging grape tangles over the gunwales. Probing ahead with an oar, I feel my way back along the river's edge. There is a fallen tree in the dark water that I ease my way through, a half-step at a time, being careful not to hole my waders.

My father extends his hand and helps me up the bank. He has set up our folding stools behind some low sumac five yards back from the bank. He works some imaginary stickiness out of the action of his automatic, and I test out my call with a few tentative clucks and quacks, then we settle down to the quiet business of waiting. I check my watch, not because I suspect that it is anywhere near shooting time, but because the first symptoms of the opening day butterflies have begun. If they ever stop, so will I. Under the clear sky, things will brighten up early, and I'll check my watch a dozen more times during the next half-hour. Our conversation is in low tones.

"Is the boat okay?"

"I tied it under some overhanging vines."

"Coffee?"

"Sure." At this time of the day, coffee is something felt as much as tasted, and it feels good. I rest the rim of the cup against my bottom lip, blowing through the swirling steam as I stare out at my decoy spread.

"The rig looks good," my father whispers.

I nod a thanks. The silhouettes of the teal and mallard decoys are still dark and colorless, but they *do* look good. Daylight will reveal a fresh paint job on each bird; rich browns and grays, crisp blacks, pure whites, iridescent greens. A season of use will wash and scuff the colors, and they'll never seem as fresh as this opening day. But today all is new; the guns show no signs of rust, my dad's "Father's Day" waders wear no patches, and even the brass heads showing in the shell box are shiny.

The sky grows lighter, and with it patches of fog begin to accumulate over the water. Across the river, several birches dressed in autumn amber emerge from the dark background of the woodland. When I can definitely see the color on the head of the nearest decoy, I check my watch and find that the season officially began more than a minute ago. I take a deep breath and flex my shoulder blades. Next to me, my father pulls back the bolt of his gun a half-inch, knowing full well there is a shell in the chamber but taking a small comfort from just seeing it there—nervous preliminaries.

We wait.

"Okay . . ." I've seen them. There is no need to say more. My father eases forward, crouching, and slowly turns to face the direction my eyes indicate.

The flock of ducks is silhouetted against the brightening dawn. They move quickly, and seem to be showing off their maneuvering skills. Teal. We lose them momentarily when they pass in front of the dark background, but they break the sky again much closer to us. There is no doubting their intentions—they come straight for the rig, skimming over the wisps of fog on the river.

The safety on my father's gun clicks off. . . .

7:50 A.M. I've never before seen a whitecap on the swamp creek, but there's no denying it now. Close behind it is another, and out farther several more waves have their tops blown back upon themselves. In the shallow lee of a broken-down black willow, our eight decoys occupy half of the small triangle of calm water. If it were winter, this would be called a blizzard instead of a typical November storm.

We had brought enough decoys to lure the entire Atlantic flyway, but thankfully we'd come to our senses in the gale winds before dawn and had put out only a handful. Chasing down storm-dragged decoys is no fun, especially when ducks are flying, and on a perfect day like this, a waterfowler needs little more than to be near some sheltered water. Shooting in the gale is difficult, but we are getting plenty of practice.

The season has waxed full. The migrants are in, as attested to by the wide variety of birds that have attempted to join our eight black duck decoys behind the willow. The only redhead duck I've ever seen in this state lies on the sacks of extra decoys behind us. My eyes keep wandering to the drake, as if in disbelief.

A small flock of mallards, flying low with the wind behind them, swings around the willow. When they see the calm water they turn outward, climbing into the wind as they look the rig over. Two hens peel away from the group, heading farther downriver, but the rest sideslip toward us, their formation scattered. Heading into the strong wind, the birds are actually flying sideways and backward as they approach. The shot is confusing at best, and we both miss. In the gale, the mallards only have to think about flaring and they are instantly out of range. No second shots are possible.

We grin foolishly at each other and reload. There is more luck than skill involved in this sort of shooting, and misses need no excuse. We hunker back down into the rushes. The wind begins to spit tiny bits of ice along with the sparse raindrops.

I've read descriptions comparing the sound to ripping canvas, but those are from a time when duck hunters were full-time watermen on whom a strain-burst sail left a lasting impression. To me, the five buffleheads sound like an F4 accelerating close overhead after a bombing run. As with the watermen, the sound leaves a lasting impression. The buffs pass behind us, braking with an alarming din as they swing across the wind to come in lightly in the rough water beyond the rig. All five are drakes. They seem to sit on the water rather than in it, seemingly inflated imitations. Their crisp coloration and bright blue bills do little to dispel the impression.

We watch them intently as they swim into the rig. My partner cups a hand to his mouth and leans toward me to have his whisper heard in the wind. "This doesn't sound too macho, but they're really cute."

I nod. They are.

"What now?" he asks.

I glance out at the little black-and-white ducks. They have fluffed out their feathers and are resting at the rear of the rig. "Let's wait for more mallards."

He grins, and nods in agreement.

11:25 A.M. We watch a hovering insect land on the knee of my waders. "A mosquito. Amazing."

My brother shakes his head. "This is crazy. November duck hunting is supposed to look like a Chet Reneson watercolor. I'm half tempted to take off my shirt and get some sun."

Late November brings an abundance of waterfowl to coastal New England, even as the inland migration begins to wane. Dawn had brought fast shooting, but the tide and the unpredictable weather has left us stranded on the sunny salt marsh for at least another hour. We wait, talking the talk of idle hunters everywhere; tomorrow's game in Foxboro, stories about our father, speculations about where the ducks are and how well we'd be doing if we were there with them.

Then, because we have not paid attention for a sufficient number of minutes, a single black duck appears over the decoys. He is a rich brown loam color in the sunlight. Without announcement I stand and pump two quick shots at the bird, and although he sags noticeably, he does not fall. Instead, he flies a straight line out onto the salt flats, losing altitude as if the load of shot had not so much injured him as weighed him down.

We stand, shading our eyes. Although we never actually see the duck fall, when he finally sinks from view we assume he's down. My brother estimates the distance: "He's weynafug out there."

I nod. "Probably farther."

After a moment's thought, he brightens and turns to me, his hand on my shoulder. "Well, for once I'm glad you saw him first." He grins. Overeagerness has its accompanying penance: Although it had been his turn to shoot, I am the one with the hike across the marsh in front of me.

I start off and am halfway across the shallow tidal creek when my brother whistles "bobwhite." I freeze . . . wait . . . then hear a single gunshot and see two teal flare off. A third is at the center of a ring of ripples just outside the decoy spread. He floats on his back with one gray foot idly paddling the air. The damsel of fate who controls the fortunes of waterfowlers must be a sadistic old biddy. She keeps score, and extracts penalties for specific transgressions: Cripple a duck and pay by watching your brother kill cleanly a bird it would have been your turn to take. She's the same one who sends in the mallards when you're picking up after a fruitless morning.

My brother waves to me. "Hurry back!" There is more than the necessary amount of glee in his voice.

The muck on the far bank of the creek is exceptionally sticky. This must be part of my penance, too. Waders should come equipped with handles just above the heels—I'm always afraid I'll puncture them by pulling as hard as I have to to get my feet out of the mud.

Up on the flats, the summertime expanse of waving grass has been turned into a stubble field. The tides and winds of autumn sweep over the marsh and carry off the deciduous plant tops, leaving only short stems that are devoid of all resiliency. I crunch along through the brittle stubble, leaping the smaller cuts as best I can in my cumbersome waders and taking the long way around the wider channels through the marsh.

At high tide the salt flats are dotted with ponds. But they drain out with the ebb, leaving empty mud holes that contain nothing more than a puddle or two. My black is in the weeds at the edge of one such drained salt pond, and he springs into flight at my approach. He gives only the slightest indication that he is an injured bird. My shooting, never anything to write home about, is poorer than usual today: I fire once too quickly, then concentrate and center him with the second shot. The bird falls into the mud, but immediately rights himself and runs for the far weedy edge, waddling like some target duck in a shooting gallery. The pellets of my third shot strike all around him, but to complete the shooting gallery simile, he rolls over only to pop back up again and resume his escape. I fumble in my pocket and bring out another shell in time to reload and fire again, but the results are exactly the same. A walking duck, of course, is not nearly as vulnerable a target as a bird in flight, and my shots have evidently not penetrated the armor that is his folded wings.

As the bird runs, so do I, trying all the while to keep the gun loaded and retain my footing on the slippery mud bank. At last I succeed in falling. When I look up, the bird has made it into the weeds. I mark the spot in my mind. But to get there, I must navigate around several cuts in the marsh. I arrive at "the spot" but am no longer sure I know where it is. Weeds and cuts have a sameness to them, especially when viewed from a different angle. Davy Crockett ponders the problem for a moment, then looks for tracks. In the soft mud they are easy to find. There is blood among the webbed footprints.

But the surface is harder in the weeds and the telltale tracks vanish. I look for feathers or blood or any other signs of the duck; there are none to be found. I search farther in. The bird has been hit four times: He cannot be all that healthy, and must be hiding nearby. I look farther up the cut, then into the next one. Protected from the winds and tides, the dead marsh grass around the drained pond is still knee high. It isn't all that thick, but a black duck has the perfect camouflage for this stuff.

Ten minutes pass, then fifteen. I look back at my brother. His estimate of the distance was accurate.

The duck is going to die before morning. It seems a waste. Before giving up, I return and look again at the duckprints leading into the tall weeds. It seems a hopeless case, but I give Davy Crockett one last hearing. Squatting down like a golfer looking over a putt, I have a different perspective. There, as obvious as a finger mark on newly brushed suede, is my own trail through the marsh grass. And that of the wounded duck.

Eight feet into the weeds, the hidden path ends. I stare at the lump of mud for a long moment before I can see the mottled khaki bill and the shape of the bird's head hunched into his breast feathers.

At times like this, looking a live cripple straight in the eye, I wish more than anything else that I had shot slightly better . . . or slightly worse.

3:15 P.M. The dull yellow-gray of the high overcast sky is typical of New England winter days. There is no warmth, no brightness, no shadow from the thin sunlight. It is as if the December sun has all it can manage to simply illuminate the afternoon landscape. In the peculiar silence of times preceding a snowfall, each sound is magnified and thrown back at us from the woodline bordering the swamp. The new ice on the marsh will hold no weight today and breaks noisily, but the cold is such that within a week all but the swiftest flowing waters will be frozen solid. Inland waterfowling is in its waning days.

We tow our boat through the ice, then hide it in some flooded puckerbrush next to the open water created by a spring hole. The crescent of brush accommodates the boat as if it had been planted with that purpose in mind. In the spring hole I arrange a late-season rig of blacks, scuffed and in need of repainting, with a pair of baldpates thrown in for color.

With the solstice just two weeks away, sunset will come early. There is barely two hours of daylight left when we settle in and begin waiting. My shins hurt from being repeatedly knocked against the shelf ice on the way in. In my pocket, the latest in my extensive collection of handwarmers has quit working. In that respect, it is little different from all the others I own.

The quiet of the marsh is complete. The insects that buzzed and hummed a backdrop through the warmer months are silenced now, and there are no bird sounds save the occasional distant cawing of a crow. No breeze stirs the few remaining leaves. My partner feels the silence too, for he barely speaks above a whisper. "I saw a few flying out of here this morning. No reason to think they shouldn't be coming back to feed this afternoon."

"That'd be nice." I speak quietly as well. "You know, just once I'd like to be able to know ahead of time that we were going to have a gangbuster's day. That way, we could shoot selectively and not have the feeling that the first hen to show up might be the only thing we'd see all day."

"This might be it, with the snow on the way and things freezing up all over . . ." He ponders his own statement for a moment, then smiles inwardly. "Could be . . ."

There has been no agreement made, but minutes later neither of us makes a move when a pair of hen mallards circles the rig, then eases in among the decoys. Conversation stops. We don't want to do anything to scare off these volunteers in our decoy regiment. The pair wanders along the edge of our spring hole, muttering duckily as they feed on buttonbush seed balls.

Within minutes, my partner nudges me and nods toward a tall pine we have been using as a reference point. I search the sky and finally notice a flock coming down the marsh, much higher than my eyes had been focused. They pass in front of us, perhaps fifteen birds altogether. There are several black ducks mixed in with what appears to be a flock of mallards. I sweet talk to them with the call, but the only answers I get are from the visitors in our decoys. The flock makes the circuit of our end of the swamp; down into the frozen corner, around the meadow behind us, then back to our pocket of open water. They are low enough on the second pass for me to clearly tell the drake mallards from the hens.

Out in the black water, the decoys are the only color in the gray December landscape. The iridescent green wing and face patches of the two baldpates seem especially gaudy among the washed-out tones of the marsh. Sixty yards from the boat, the two suzies continue to feed, paddling about and clucking softly. When one of them rears back and stretches her wings, I know the circling flock is ours.

They pass behind us for the fourth time. My ears follow the sound of air through their wings, and my eyeballs strain at the tops of their sockets. The birds appear below the brim of my downtilted hat, banking around on their final approach.

Next to me, my partner takes a deep breath.

With cupped wings and extended feet, the flock begins its flip-flopping descent; gray bodies, white wing linings, iridescent speculums against the dull winter sky.

We shoulder our guns together, eyes skyward.

5:50 P.M. Coming back with the drone of the motor filling my ears, I wonder why the night is thought of as black: The sky and water are shades of cobalt and purple and ultramarine, and the passing shoreline is shadowed in tones of indigo. Some of the sky colors blend and change and darken even as I watch, but nowhere is there a color I can label as black. The water mysteriously continues to hold the twilight glow, even though the sky and landscape grow darker. Over the darkening treetops, the Dipper is at its low winter point, nearly touching the horizon. The first stars of Cygnus the Swan shine in the west above the lavender line that was the sunset.

Mine is the only boat returning. There are no other gunners out on this last day of the season. Even the bats and snipe that amused me on other, earlier evenings are absent, having headed for warmer climates. The season—which began with teal and native wood ducks on this same river, then waxed full during first the inland and then the coastal migrations, and finally brought in the late redlegs in its waning days—has ended. Blacks will be the local natives for the next few months. For some reason known only to themselves, they choose to remain on what little water stays open through the bitter New England winter. Two of their number lay on the sacks of decoys in the bow. They are impressive trophies on the wing, but right now look for all the world like a couple of dead cats—nothing is rattier looking than a dead duck that has spent a few hours in the bilges of a boat.

The reprieve from the cold that came with picking up and sacking the decoys is fading. I jam my hands deeper into the pockets of my parka, then finally hug them into my armpits and use my knee to steer the boat through the blue evening.

The work of hauling the boat onto the trailer goes quickly. I carry the gas can and the motor to the back of the truck, then use a hand lantern to check for things that might have been forgotten in the shadows. My fingers are so numb that I cannot push the switch to shut off the light. Normally, I am eager to be out of my waders and on my way toward home and supper, but on this last night of the season, I linger. I toss the lantern into the cab, then reach in and shut off the headlights and the engine. In spite of my cold feet and fingers, I walk back to the edge of the river. One last time before the season slips completely into the past, I want to listen to the silence and see again the stars reflected in the quiet water.

Mike's Dog

WHILE STRAIGHTENING OUT a few things in my corner of the cellar, I happened to bump the peg where the dogs' hunting collars were hung. The attached bells tinkled softly, and although it was 10 p.m. on the snowiest night of February, both dogs were instantly at my feet, dancing with expectation. Pavlov first documented it, but anyone who has ever owned a hunting dog knows the association dogs quickly make with anything connected to "going out": Pull on your boots before venturing out to shovel the driveway or check over your shotgun in preparation for a trip to the skeet range and the dogs are there, trembling with excitement and asking questions with their eyes. The association isn't limited to inanimate things, either: Let your hunting partner show up for a night of poker and beer and even a sleeping dog is quickly in second gear at the sound of his voice.

My friend Mike tells of a dog he once had as a boy in Pennsylvania. "He was just a mongrel, but damned if he wasn't the *smartest* dog I've ever known. I'd get down my little Fox 20 side-by and he'd know right away what we were doin'—he'd head straight for the alders and start huntin' birds. And if I'd get out my father's 12-gauge automatic, he'd watch the sky for ducks. When he saw me carryin' the .22, he'd hunt nothin' but rabbits and squirrels, and he knew the .30-30 meant he should run deer. He was smart. Why, one day I got out my fishin' rod, and when I looked for that dog, he was out in the yard diggin' worms."

Mike was good. He never cracked a smile until after the last line.

Remnants

SEATED ON the fallen birch, he tugged at the loose bark on the trunk. A piece tore away easily, and he crumbled it in his small mitten. Next to him, his father glanced at his activities and slid his free arm around the boy's shoulders.

"Are you cold, Joey?"

The boy shook his head, but snuggled closer under the protecting arm. His father cradled the big gun so effortlessly in his other arm that Joey wondered if he might have been mistaken when he concluded that it was too heavy for him to lift.

"Maybe we'll see some ducks pretty soon." His father spoke in thickly accented tones without looking at him. *"Are you looking in the sky down by the river there?"*

Joey watched, but in a minute grew tired of the uneventful vista and returned to peeling birch bark from his seat. The warm smell that was his father intermingled with the aroma of cigarette tobacco and the musty odor of the canvas shooting coat. He remembered reaching as high as he could to feel in the pockets of the coat where it hung in the front hall closet, and now he slid his hand into the big flapped pocket and found the mysterious cartridges.

"Hands cold?" His father smiled down at him.

After a moment the boy took out one of the shotgun shells and turned it over in his hands. He took off his mitten and ran his thumbnail along the ribs of the green case, and felt how cold the brass head seemed. There was a yellow piece of paper stuck onto the opposite end of the shell. On it was printed a number Joey recognized.

"Look, Daddy . . . Four."

"Uh-huh." His father nodded and smiled briefly, then returned his gaze to the brightening sky.

He read the letters printed on the side of the shell: "Daddy, what does R-E-M-I-N-G-T-O-N spell?"

"Remington."

"Oh." After a short pause, he asked, "What does K-L-E-E-N-B-O-R-E spell?"

His father cut him off. *"Hold on, Joey . . . There's some coming."* His father crouched lower on the log.

"Some what, Daddy?"

"Ducks. See 'em? Look down by the river."

"Those birds flying?"

"Uh-huh. Just watch now . . ."

He hunkered low on his seat in an imitation of his father. The ducks came toward them, intent on the swamp pond immediately behind their hiding place, looming ever larger in the dull sky. When Joey was looking nearly straight up, his father stood and raised the gun and fired twice. The boy tried to keep his eyes on the birds, but at the sound of his father's gun, the pieces of paper wadding from the shells filled the sky overhead. The illusion was that the small flock of ducks had split into dozens of separate forms, each going in a different direction. Confused, he watched the black forms grow smaller while one grew ever larger, not seeming to fall until, after a long moment, it whistled down to land behind them with a thump.

"Stay right here," said his father, and started off into the high grass. After he stared at the sky, it seemed dark when Joey looked down. At the edge of the area where the grass was trampled down, he spied something that hadn't been there a moment before. He eased forward on the birch log until his feet touched the ground, and went to pick up the empty shell. A wisp of smoke came from its mouth. Out of curiosity he bent his head to sniff the new odor.

"Did you see that, Joey?" There was excitement in his father's voice. He was holding a duck by the foot.

"Uh-huh." The boy nodded his head.

His father beamed, and opened the duck's wing to display the iridescent speculum. Joey looked up at the sky, still unsure of what he had seen: A few feathers floated in the air, and a single wind-blown leaf spun spirals as it drifted by. His father lifted him onto the birch log again and sat down beside the boy.

"I'm thinking maybe more will come soon. We'll see."

Joey absently held the empty shell to his nose again.

WHEN THE MUSIC stopped, he automatically pushed the "eject" button and flipped the tape over. Before he could reinsert the cassette, Colleen asked idly, "What else have you got to listen to?"

Joseph smiled to himself and opened the lid of the storage console between the seats. "Help yourself . . . nothing that'll wake up the dog, though." He indicated the springer spaniel dozing on the floor of the car at Colleen's feet. She chose a title after a moment's study, then paused to look closely at the cassette before slipping it into the slot in the deck.

"You really are methodical: I'll bet you always rewind your tapes."

Joseph didn't take his eyes from the road as the car wound around an uphill turn. "One of my faults—I'll be more slovenly in the future."

She persisted. "No, really . . . Didn't anyone ever tell you how organized you are? Everything you do is that way. I'll bet all the bills in your wallet are in a nice neat stack, all face front."

He laughed. "Good strategy—marry 'em first, then go for his wallet."

"Am I right?"

"Of course. But what does that prove?"

She smiled smugly and popped the tape into the slot. Her finger hovered over the "play" button. "What about me, Mister Methodical? If you know me so well, what tape did I just pick?"

"Rachmaninoff."

"Cute." Rachmaninoff was what he had just played. "Come on—which of your tapes would I have chosen?"

After a long pause, he announced, "Fleetwood Mac."

"You *saw* it before I put it in, didn't you!"

He laughed out loud.

Their car scattered the fallen leaves as it passed. Overnight the wind had sculpted the remnants of last summer's shade like wind-blown snow drifts across the road, but the passing of the first car changed the illusion, pushing up a restless wake of leaves behind it. Even though the leaf fall was nearly complete throughout the Berkshires, an occasional roadside maple retained its foliage, incandescently glowing in the horizontal morning light and all the more spectacular for its lack of competition.

The road paralleled a shallow valley where abandoned fields were growing to gray birch and popple. At the end of the road, tucked into the morning shadow of the climbing hills beyond, was what remained of an old farmhouse. The windows had gone the way of all things breakable, the roof had fallen in in several places, and the lilacs that once guarded the front steps now grew through the porch roof. Beyond, partially hidden by a thicket of sumac, stood a barn. As if in direct contrast to its companion, it appeared serviceable in every way. Only its surroundings belied the presumption that hay bales might not still be stored in its loft, awaiting the New England winter.

Joseph eased the car into the old driveway and shut off the engine. "We're here."

"Where's 'here'?"

"The Boskiewiczs' farm, or at least what used to be their farm. Look . . ." He pointed through the windshield to where a doe and her nearly grown fawn stood in the orchard fifty yards away, staring at them. Colleen pushed the "stop" button, silencing Stevie Nicks for the moment. The deer stood immobile, staring at the car. Only their tails and ears flicked occasionally. "They wouldn't have lasted long if old man Boskiewicz was still around. He didn't care what time of the year it was—deer meant venison to him."

"He was a poacher?"

Joseph paused. "He was a farmer. Deer ate his corn, he ate the deer. Living hand-to-mouth gives people a different perspective. I don't think he ever thought of himself as a poacher." After a moment he added, "Most of his neighbors did, though."

At Colleen's feet, the springer whined impatiently. She reached down and petted the dog. The doe finally grew uneasy and, after nibbling a last apple, turned and disappeared into the brush. The fawn followed.

Joseph opened the car door and the little dog nearly pushed him out of the way, then made running circuits of the car as he gathered the gear they'd need for the morning. Still in the store bag with the receipt stapled across the top was the box of shells Joseph had bought the day before. "Dove & Quail Loads," the box read. He took the time to fill each set of shell loops inside the pockets of his father's old hunting jacket. He was disappointed that the shells were not green.

Full of energy, the dog raced in front of them as they entered an old pasture. The land was still fenced but long forgotten. Several brooklets flowed out of the hills behind the farm, joining to form the stream that defined the bottom of the valley. Frost still clung to the grasses and low bushes in the shadow of the tree line, but melted away darkly where the slanting sunlight reached the ground. The illusion was of a white shadow, a preview of winter days to come. The dog was quickly soaked from the melted frost, as were their pantlegs.

Ahead of them, the dog put her nose to the ground and skidded to a stop. She seemed a hovering bumblebee: Whatever energy had gone into locomotion now went into tail wagging. She stopped, then scurried back and forth until she had relocated whatever it was she had been sniffing, then dashed ahead again only to stop just as suddenly. Her stub tail was a blur of excited motion.

Joseph approached with his gun at port arms. Colleen stood back, not sure of what to expect. A pair of mourning doves fluttered up into the bare lower branches of a streamside alder, then, seeing Joseph, took wing and sailed farther down the tree line. As they passed, more doves took wing from the edge of the brook, and those, in turn, stirred up even more with their passing.

He turned to say something to Colleen, but smiled when he saw her with her hands over her ears. He whistled to the dog and waved her across the field toward a stand of popples. "She'll be mousing around with those doves all day if I let her—it looks like there's a whole flight of them in along the brook." After a pause, he said, "You've never heard a shotgun?"

She shook her head.

"It says 'bang.'" He grinned. "Actually, more like 'ka-BLAM,' but the noise won't bother you so long as you're behind the gun rather than next to it."

"It looks like it'd knock you over."

"This was my father's gun. They make gas-powered automatics now that you can shoot off of your nose, but not this old lady." The gun he held out was a well-used version of the classic square-backed automatic, its checkering worn smooth and its blueing replaced by a silvered patina from years of handling. "It's an old Browning. It's got a sort of double-shuffle recoil that isn't too bad once you get used to it. But, yes, it kicks. It's a duck gun, really, but I had the choke opened up."

Her blank stare told him what he had said meant nothing to her. *Gas-powered automatics, Brownings, chokes*—it was enough that it was a *gun*. Guns were something a girl from the city feared, and her fear was untempered by any sort of fascination. Up until just a few days ago, shotguns had not been a part of her image of him. He wondered how else that had changed in recent days. He thought back to the previous afternoon:

> The springer had been standing on the porch steps, barking at them as they drove up. Joseph got out and spoke to the dog, *"Siedz i stul pysk."* The little springer sat down and was quiet. "She doesn't understand English," he explained. "She's my mother's dog."
>
> Colleen smiled, but said nothing.
>
> Joseph's mother was a laughing woman who, although she had no accent, conversed with the halting quality of someone who was translating in her mind as she spoke. Outwardly, she welcomed Colleen, but continually deferred to her son:
>
> "Would your wife like more coffee?"
>
> "She's right there, Ma—ask her."
>
> During supper there was family talk of uncles and cousins and crops and whose farm had been sold off. Joseph noticed Colleen's poise never faltered under the examining eye of his mother: *Of course she was younger than Joe, but that was something other people seemed to worry about more than they did.* Not bad. Yes, *kapusta* tasted

just as Joe had described it. Hey, she's fast on her feet. *No, her parents were in Florida. She had shared an apartment in the city with a friend before they were married.* With a *friend!* Whew!

Afterward, he busied himself in the kitchen, assembling his stored hunting gear while the two women stood at the sink with the dishes. The forced nature of their small talk only seemed to underline the fact that mother-in-law and daughter-in-law were complete strangers in virtually every way, but Colleen tried her best to fill in the gaps. Finally, after an uncomfortably long silence, Joseph's mother said, "Such a long time I waited to meet you, and now that you are here, I sometimes don't know to say the right things." The woman averted her eyes as she spoke, drying her hands on a dish towel. There was a puzzled look on Colleen's face: She had known Joseph barely six months, hardly a 'long time.' Finally, Joseph's mother added, "All these years, meeting Joey's girlfriends—it's good, at last, to meet the one he makes his wife."

Overhearing this, Joseph laughed. "Ma, you make it sound like I've been parading an endless bunch of women up here for years." He turned to Colleen, shaking his head in mock disgust. "Every time I'd bring a girl up here, Ma would check out her legs to see if she could pull a plow. 'This one's a real *pani,* Joey—good for pretty, but not for strong.' None of them ever met Ma's approval."

They all laughed, but there followed a poignant moment when Joseph's mother put her arm around Colleen's shoulders and said, somewhat embarrassed, "Until now, Joey."

All through the uncomfortable evening, Colleen had represented herself well. Later, her only comment to Joseph was, "So I'm the end result of 'years of Joey's girlfriends.' Mister Meticulous, indeed."

JOSEPH'S PERCEPTION of himself changed whenever he returned to the Berkshires. It was far more complicated than just becoming someone who owned a shotgun. He tried for a moment to see himself through Colleen's eyes but found he could not focus on just himself. In the city, he saw himself more clearly. Here, there was so much about this place that was a part of him that he wasn't sure he could ever separate one from the other.

They entered the grove of aspens along the far edge of the field. The ground beneath them was littered with recently fallen leaves that seemed to create their own light, brightening the scene from an unusual angle. Joseph paused a moment. "Isn't this lovely?" He held a single aspen leaf for a moment before offering it to Colleen. It was delicate and unblemished, a clear, almost-translucent yellow, and the longer Colleen looked at the leaf, the more obvious its loveliness became.

In front of them, the little black-and-white springer searched the stand of popples. Near the end of the grove, she struck scent and narrowed her casts. The speed of her tail increased proportionally. At the end of the grove, she bounded ahead into a run of blackberries. Joseph whistled and said, *"Stój!"* and the dog sat and waited for them to catch up.

They walked the outside edge of the blackberry bushes while the dog worked in among them, seemingly impervious to the thorns. A woodcock appeared above the tops of the bushes and was gone so quickly that Joseph was left wondering if it was ever there in the first place. Neither the dog nor Colleen paused.

"Did you see that?"

"What?"

"I guess you didn't. The dog bumped a woodcock." He started into the thicket, whistling to the dog as he went. "Let's make a little circle in here—sometimes there's more than one . . ."

Almost immediately, the dog pushed up a pair of birds. Just as the first woodcock had done, they climbed only to the top of the shoulder-high blackberries, then made flank turns and headed for the wooded hillside. Joseph fired quickly at the nearer of the two, but the shot was missed before he pulled the trigger. He switched off and fired twice more at the second bird as it twisted through a white pine, but his shots only brought down a sprinkle of dead pine needles. He shook his head, smiling to himself.

After a moment, Colleen asked, "What did you see?"

"You didn't see those two, either? The dog put them out—two more woodcock."

"Tell me what I'm looking for."

"Woodcock are nifty little birds . . . Hell, I've got a picture of a couple on the wall of my office—you've seen it."

"I thought those were hummingbirds."

"Hummingbirds?" He laughed in surprise. "Did you think the other picture was a pair of chickens in an apple tree?"

"Hey, I don't know about these hunting things. Before I met you the only birds I recognized were pigeons and bats—and I knew enough to stay away from both." She caught him laughing. "What's so funny?"

"Not a thing. But you're right: Pigeons and bats have been known to have poor personal hygiene habits." Joseph tried to hide his amusement.

"Are you laughing at me?"

"No." He was.

The springer came in, and Colleen knelt to pet her. "You're a good girl." The dog smiled an open-mouthed dog's smile at her. "Find us some more woodcocks, and make sure they fly where I can see them." She glanced at Joseph before adding, "While you're at it, see if you can make them slow down a bit, too. Buffalo Bill there seems to be having a little trouble today."

Joseph shook his head. "You're wasting your time—she doesn't speak English." He waved his arm in an underhand motion, and whistled and said, *"Pospiesz sie!"* The springer broke away from Colleen at his command and cast out in front, hunting as intently as before. They followed after her.

"What did you tell the dog?" she asked.

"I said, 'Don't pay any attention to that bimbo; she doesn't know a woodcock from a woodpecker.'"

They both laughed.

AT NOON they stopped along the stream to eat the lunch they had brought with them. The morning had warmed into a blue-sky New England day, and the sunlight filtered brightly through the bare branches of the birches overhead. The springer stood in the shallows, alternately lying down to cool her belly then standing to vigorously shake off the water.

Colleen watched the shifting play of shadows on the stream. She still had the aspen leaf that Joseph had given to her. It seemed to represent a part of life that she had missed, or at least had never taken notice of. "It's lovely here," she said. There had been an absence of dialogue throughout their lunch. "In your mind, do you still think of this as 'home'?"

He fed the remains of his sandwich to the dog before he answered. "Physically, you can move away from a place like this, but I guess it'll always be home to me."

"Would you ever want to move back here?"

He shook his head. "When I left here years ago, I did it on purpose."

"You've said that before. Why?" When he didn't answer, she filled in the silence. "Joe, I need to see this through your eyes. We came up here so I could meet your family and so they could get a look at Joey's new wife, and that's fine. But more than that, I was looking forward to finding out where you came from and who you used to be so that I could understand a little more about who you are now."

Seated on the fallen birch, he absently pulled at the loose bark. At length he said, "These old-country farm people up here don't say, 'Hi, how are ya?'—they say, *'Co robisz?'* which literally translates to

'What work are you doing?' You've got to understand that this is more than just a *place:* This is a way of life—one that can trap a person. Evidently, my father had that in pretty clear focus, and wanted me to know that there was more to life than tobacco farming and digging potatoes and working yourself into an early grave. 'Education,' he told my mother, not that he even realized himself all it could give. So here I am; the son of an immigrant, the first person with my last name to hold a high school diploma, let alone a college degree. As proud of me as my mother is—she talks about her son the CPA to anyone who'll listen—she's a part of this too, and she's secretly waiting for the day when I'll see the light and come home to run the farm." He paused, listening to his own thoughts for a moment, then added, "It's my father's dream that I'm living out in a place away from here."

"Do you remember him at all?"

Joseph shook his head. "People tell me I look like my father, that I've got his temperament. He was. . . ," he smiled at Colleen, ". . . meticulous. But he died before I was five years old. I've searched all through my memories—thousands of times—I've looked hard, but I cannot find one single memory of him. Everything I know about him comes through my family—and things like this." He pinched the lapel of the hunting coat that he referred to as "Dad's jacket."

THE STREAM widened as it flowed around a bend. Against the far shore, the backwash barely trickled through the shallows, but there was deep water on the outside of the curve where the brook danced over a series of submerged rocks. A few that might qualify as small boulders poked through the surface. The springer jumped into the deep water and paddled to the shallows, hardly pausing to watch the hopscotch antics of Joseph and Colleen as they tried to cross with dry feet.

There was nothing spectacular about Joseph's fall: He was on a rock one moment and then, a moment later, was standing next to it in the brook. "I did that to impress the dog." He grinned as he walked knee-deep in the stream to the boulder where Colleen stood giggling. "I was an apprentice troll at one time. Here, hop up on my back and I'll give you a lift." He carried her to the far bank and climbed out himself. Colleen was still laughing.

"On days when I remember to bring along an extra pair of socks, I never need them, and, of course, when I forget them, that's when I fall in." He untied and emptied first one boot, then the other. "But today, I've actually outsmarted myself: I left these in the coat last season—I forgot I had them." He took out an old pair of wool socks from the coat's gamebag, shook off the few feathers and twigs that clung to them, and put them on.

"That's why I married you." Colleen shook her head in amusement. "If right now I needed something—anything—a baloney sandwich or a ticket to Kalamazoo, somehow you'd have it. How do you do it?"

"You haven't seen the half of it. Stick with me, kiddo—being methodical has its rewards." He was joking, but when he looked up from lacing his boots, he was surprised to find that Colleen's expression was pensive. "Is something wrong?"

"No—there's nothing the matter." She touched his arm as she spoke. "It's what you said—I'm just now realizing that I've known that about you all along."

THE AIR smelled of fallen apples as they climbed through a stand of pines toward an overgrown orchard, following what had once been a farm road. They stopped and sat on a stone wall, catching their breaths after the uphill trudge. Wild clematis climbed among the branches of the apple trees near the wall. The white beards of its spent flowers caught the moving pattern of sunlight beneath the orchard's canopy. Without being called, the springer came in and sat at their feet. Colleen petted the dog.

"Tired?" he asked.

She nodded. "A little."

"We're already on our way back. It'll be just another half-hour or so."

When they started on again, the dog sprinted in front of them, but the morning's exercise had taken its toll on her too, and she soon slowed to a steady trot as she scouted the thickets of viburnum among the old apple trees. Most of the fruit on the ground had been gnawed or picked by some woodland animal or another, and the exposed flesh had turned brown. But Joseph noticed several apples that still showed white where their peels had been picked away within the past few minutes. At the same time, the springer came to life, racing ahead, then back again, obviously on bird scent but not able to follow it anywhere.

"What . . . ?" Colleen began, but Joseph put a finger to his lips. He stood with the shotgun at ready while the dog continued searching, her tail wagging so furiously that the springer's entire rear end wagged.

Suddenly a grouse thundered out of the next apple tree, closely followed by the sound of a second. Joseph reacted but saw only shadows through the sparse leaves. A third bird roared out above them, angling back into the sun. He pushed the gun ahead of the silhouette and fired. *Leaves and feathers flew at his shot, but in the blinding brightness he couldn't make out one form from another until one grew larger, not seeming to fall at first, but then streamed by him and landed with a thump.*

Momentarily blinded by the sun, he stood blinking for a few seconds, then looked to where the grouse had come down: The springer was already bringing the bird in, prancing to him with her head held high. *At the edge of a thatch of grass Joseph noticed something that hadn't been there a moment before. As he picked up the empty shell, a wisp of smoke came from its mouth. He glanced back up to where the shot had been made: A few feathers floated in the sunlight, and a single leaf spun spirals on the breeze as it fell.*

He smiled inwardly, thinking.

"What is it?" Colleen asked.

Joseph shook his head. "Déjà vu, I guess. Just for a moment there . . ."

The springer nudged his hand, and he knelt to take the bird from her, scratching the dog's ears as he did. He smoothed down the grouse's plumage and spread the tail fan for Colleen to see. Only one feather had been broken. "This is a grouse: not gaudy like a pheasant or a wood duck, but a handsome bird all the same." He glanced up at her.

"It looks just like one of those apple tree chickens from your office." She was teasing him, and he grinned in return.

He slid the bird into the game pocket of his coat. "I haven't done much hunting these past few seasons: This is the first grouse I've put into Dad's jacket in over two years."

"He'd have been proud of you," she said.

It seemed a natural reply to Joseph's statement, but he pondered it a moment before answering. He glanced up beyond the branches of the apple tree once again, but the air was empty now and the remnants of the image slipped away like a half-remembered dream. "I'd like to think so," he said. "I really would."

The Mousecatcher

LIKE ME, my dogs like mice. They seem to know I'm on my way to the woodpile as soon as I come out of the cellar, and race each other to the stack. There is no mistaking their excitement as they jockey for position, eyes and noses intent on the spaces between the logs as I fill the woodbox. The mice that live there fascinate them.

Some men have an ability to reduce the size of a stack of cordwood once it's split, but I don't have that puzzlemaker's knack—my woodpiles grow taller with splitting and restacking. The resulting abundance of spaces makes for a veritable tenement for mice, and as I load the woodbox, I inadvertently evict a mouse from his winter quarters.

The apparent quickness mice have on a linoleum floor is an illusion of confined space: In the open yard they scamper but are defeated by the distances involved. The setters hurtle the woodpile after the renegade; chase, pounce . . . but seldom actually catch the mouse. Each thinks the other has it under her paws. The little guy makes his escape, still scampering, often between the hind legs of his would-be captor. There are canine looks of disbelief when the mouse's absence is discovered, then the dogs do some scampering of their own. The show is far funnier than any mouse cartoon my children might watch on a Saturday morning.

Mice have never received what could be called "good press": Otherwise calm women scream in terror at their appearance. Farmers and storekeepers hate them. They are lumped in with lice, cockroaches, and rats under the label *vermin* (an evil-sounding word if ever there was one), and folks feel obliged to exterminate them. They are, after all, rodents (another evil-sounding word). Society tends to judge animals by their worth to mankind, and mice rate a flat zero. There is, after all, no market for mouse pelts. There is no demand for them in epicurean restaurants. If you scratch hard enough, someone might mention that mice eat weed seeds, but other than that, no one has a kind word for them.

Me, I like mice. I've never had any quarrel with them. The handsome fellows that live out in the woodpile pretty much mind their own business, and the little guys in the marsh that scramble around my boots while I'm duck hunting keep me entertained. The best grouse dog that I ever owned would occasionally pause to point a mouse if she could see it. Exasperating as it could be, the experience would serve to remind me that hunting is not nearly so serious a business as I sometimes make it out to be.

And what would cartoonists and writers of children's fiction do without mouse characters? Mighty Mouse. Speedy Gonzales. Jerry's Tom. Mickey himself. In a realm where mice sometimes chase cats and keep dogs for pets, only Thornton Burgess portrayed them accurately: constantly hunted by every form of predator both great and small, in a never-ending search for food, living anywhere and everywhere.

It is this last ubiquitous quality that gets them into trouble, usually in the fall when the cold forces them to move indoors. Like weeds, no one pays them much attention until they appear where they are not wanted.

I hear the garage door rumble downward, then my wife enters the house. She is talking before the door has closed behind her. "Steven, there's a mouse in the garage. I saw him in the headlights when I put the car away."

I dodge. "What'd he look like?"

"Like a mouse."

"A small fellow? With white feet and a rather long tail?"

"Don't be funny." She folds her arms and tries to look stern. "I'm not going out there again until you get rid of that mouse."

I shrug.

She plays her ace. "And the children aren't going out to empty the trash, either."

Ouch. That leaves just me and the mouse as the only ones allowed in the garage. He has to go.

Actually, I'd known all week we had a garage guest. The few sunflower seeds I had spilled while filling the bird feeder were mysteriously gone the following morning. At some time in the future, perhaps during spring cleaning, we'll move some forgotten item on the back shelf and find a nest of string and leaves and junk in which will be the hulls of the missing sunflower seeds.

Evicting a mouse calls for action. Leaving a note won't help. ("Susan saw you last night. That wasn't too smart. You'd better pack up and leave.") I once brought the dogs out there, hoping they'd sniff out the mouse and I could just shoo him out of the garage. Unfortunately, I forgot that I had baited several mousetraps with cream cheese. When I returned minutes later, my traps had caught a pair of English setters by the tongues. Those catch-'em-alive devices aren't much help. I once caught a mouse in one and brought it outside to release the little guy. He hit the ground and ran back into the garage. Next time, I brought the trap out near the woodpile before letting him out. Within two days we had a mouse in the garage again. I didn't check his uniform number, but I felt sure it was the same one. He knew the way.

So I resort to mousetraps.

All-gray house mice are rare in the country. Mostly, I catch white-footed and deer mice (I confess to not being able to tell the difference) and an occasional vole. (Thornton Burgess's Danny the Meadow Mouse was a vole.) I bait traps with bacon or peanut butter or (my setters' favorite) cream cheese, but I am not an enthusiastic trapper of mice. Yet I swat flies and mosquitoes with a vengeance. I catch trout to eat. And I hunt, fairly and sportsmanlike, never pretending that bird shooting is any fun for the birds. Perhaps it is because I hunt that I regret the necessity of my mousetraps: The mouse in my garage is seeking simple survival, doing what is right in Nature's world. Emptying a trap into the trash can, I do not think of the fact that mice are, by design, at the low end of the food chain and a necessity for predators everywhere. Nor do I reflect on the fact that it is a lucky mouse who lives long enough to see his first birthday. No. Instead, I find myself wishing that I could be like my dogs: chase, pounce, but never quite make the kill.

Maybe next year I will try leaving a note. I'll hang it on the barrel where I keep the sunflower seeds, but down low where they can see it. The print will be very tiny, but the message will be clear:

"Be smart—stay out in the woodpile!"

Pretzel Logic

HE SHUT OFF the alarm and stumbled toward the bathroom in the dark. When he finished, he stood at the window, peering out at the sky: *No stars.* That was good news, but it hardly elated him.

His wife sat up in bed, shielding her eyes from the bathroom light. "Please be careful out there, Sandy." She always said that.

"Okay, Hon. I'll see you later."

He almost wished she had said, "Don't be a fool—Come back to bed." Waking up was a challenge. He would be a much more serious duck hunter if it didn't involve getting up in the middle of the night. He felt three feet thick.

The eleven o'clock weather had shown a front bearing down on the region. *Duck weather. Maybe a chance to actually fill out the new five-bird limit.* Sandy had hurriedly assembled his gear and was in bed before midnight. There hadn't been sufficient time, though, to perform the mental trick of mustering the optimistic anticipation he would need in the morning to propel himself past his initial stupor and out into the darkness. Inertia, unfortunately, worked both ways. In the kitchen, he plugged in the coffee maker, then sat opposite the pile of clothes he had assembled the night before. Long johns. Turtle-neck sweater. Woolen bibfronts. Goose down coat. *Goose down coat? Give me a break—it's only November.* He tossed the cumbersome coat aside in favor of his shell parka.

When the coffee was ready, he filled the thermos and poured a cup for himself, then went into the cellar to let Jeff out. The springer sniffed his way around the yard, irrigating the trees and hedges as he went. Jeff was a pheasant dog and as much a duck retriever as he needed to be: He was neither stylish nor persistent, and once he left the boat, Sandy had little control over him. Occasionally he even missed a bird. But Jeff knew how to sit still. Day in, day out, that one asset made the little springer more valuable to Sandy than any of his friends' retrievers. The dog came to him now, tail wagging, eager to get started. "That water's gonna be cold, Jeff. Still want to go?" By way of reply, the springer's tail wagged even faster as he sat smiling an open-mouthed dog's smile up at Sandy. *Who says dogs take after their masters?*

Everything he would need had been loaded into the boat the previous night, and now he rolled the trailer out of the garage and hitched it to the truck. He still felt more asleep than awake as he drove off.

The weatherman had mentioned temperatures falling into the upper thirties, but it was obviously colder than that already: A skim of ice had begun to form at the water's edge as he launched the boat. The wind stirred the treetops above the launch ramp, and the air felt of rain.

With Jeff sitting on the sacks of decoys, Sandy started the outboard and headed upriver toward the place he called the swamp point. The spot's singular advantage was its inaccessibility—it couldn't be reached without a boat. There would be other waterfowlers out on this Saturday morning, and Sandy intended to avoid as much competition as he could. He looked at the luminescent hands of his watch, then at the lowering sky. *No need to hurry—dawn will be late under this overcast.*

It was almost three miles to the flooded point. It loomed in the darkness as a shapeless silhouette, with a stretch of sheltered water beyond. Sandy played his light along the shore, as much to signal any other hunters as to get his bearings. No lights flashed in return. Jeff stood in the bow, watching as the decoys were tossed out. "What'll it be today, Jeff—the crescent pattern? Or the two-group arrangement?" The dog kept his opinion to himself.

When he pulled the boat into the flooded brush, a branch caught against his thigh, and as he pulled away, it tore the fabric of his waders. He ran his fingers into the rip, cursing under his breath. For a moment he considered the roll of tape in his bag, but remembered past experiences of trying to persuade adhesive to stick to cold canvas and decided not to bother.

The wind whispered in the naked branches of the alders and oaks along the shoreline, sending an occasional dead leaf swirling darkly past his decoys. Without seeming to grow brighter, the sky became less black. Two of his decoys had become tangled and were floating side by side. He took the broken hockey stick he used as a wading staff and, very much aware of the tear in his waders, walked into the shallows to separate the pair.

He had left the thermos on the kitchen counter—that realization came to him as he felt for it in his war bag. Then he opened his shellbox and realized that he was in the midst of a bad-luck morning. He shook his head. "What next . . .?" Instead of his three-inch number 4s, he had mistakenly grabbed the box with the light 6s he used for pheasants. He searched into the pockets of his parka, but it was 6s or nothing. He fed three of the shells into his pumpgun. *Hunters killed ducks for years with loads like these*, he told himself. But he knew too that confidence was a big part of successful shooting, and the magnum 4s he favored weren't doing him any good back on the shelf in the garage.

As the dawn turned the clouds successively paler shades of gray, his eyes were continually drawn to a stump beyond the decoys that pretended to be a swimming duck. Legal shooting time came and went, marked only by a flurry of shots in the distance. "Chase 'em down this way," he muttered.

A half-hour later, he noticed the first raindrops in the water. He tugged at the hood on his parka, pulling it up over his cap. Sandy missed the coffee he would be pouring at this point. He editorialized on the day so far: *Rain, bum luck, no ducks*—he shook his head. *Maybe I should heed the signs and quit right now: Bad-luck mornings have a way of continuing on until they become absolutely lousy days.* The series of expanding circles in the water began to overlap as the rain quickened.

Another barrage sounded out in the distance. It was fully an hour into legal shooting time now. "We can't go home skunked, Jeff. If I can get just one shot, I'll be happy." The dog glanced at him, then returned his gaze to the treetops. In the distance, more shots thudded dully. The springer whined with impatience.

Without warning, a single drake mallard appeared. Sandy hadn't seen the bird approach—it was suddenly just *there*, backpedaling as it eased down over the spread. Caught unaware, he felt like a sprinter who hears the starter's gun as he's fitting his spikes into the blocks. His shot missed. He rushed to fire again, and then a third time. Only his empty shells hit the water.

The duck was gone so quickly he wasn't sure it was ever really there. He looked back over the decoys, but no feathers floated on the water or in the air. "What the *hell* is wrong with me?" It was more an accusation than a question. He sat back down. *A gift shot like that . . .* He pushed his hood back. *I might as well get wet, because I can't hear with that thing over my head.* ". . . Can't see, either," he muttered. An easy miss required an excuse: It was the hood. A few big ragged snowflakes began to mix in with the rain. He tucked his hands into his armpits and sat hunched forward with the barrel of the shotgun resting on the gunwale of the boat. He watched the flow of the river past the decoys. The sparse parade of leaves it carried were mostly oaks this late in the season. His head shook in disgust each time he re-played the muffed shot.

A small knot of ducks appeared in the distance, working the river. *Call? They're not talking to me, though.* His duck call was in his pocket, but Sandy's rule was to speak only when spoken to. He decided to let his decoys do all the work. After two circuits of the area, the ducks disappeared over the tree line, apparently without having seen his rig. *Should've called 'em,* he thought.

Minutes later, the same flock was back and began working the river again, this time toward the swamp point. *Call now? They're coming right for me this time.* Indecision haunted him. He hunkered lower on the thwart. There were five birds. He mentally rehearsed the shots he would need to make if he was to take more than just a single.

The ducks set their wings as they approached the decoys, but then, instead of circling, they swung out over the river as if they intended to fly on. He gritted his teeth. *Damn! Why didn't I take them when I had the chance?* The echoes of that thought were still in his mind when he saw the flock returning, banking into their final descent. Automatically, he stood and fired—much too soon—but only drew feathers from the lead drake. The birds climbed out of range. Like a golfer throwing his club after a bad drive, he pumped two more shots out, then watched as the drake lagged behind the others as they made their way back downriver.

"YOU JACKASS!" he yelled, and a moment later the echo of his frustration repeated his accusation. *Sit out here for two hours, then don't even know enough to wait 'em out when the time comes.* He worked the action of the gun to put a shell into the chamber. *If I had fours . . .* He turned the gun over and jammed two shells into the magazine, then squinted up into the drizzle where the shot had taken place. *It's my shooting, not the shells.* He shook his head. *Six empties and the only duck I've hit is still flying. Stupid.* Like a comforting friend, Jeff left his seat in the bow and came to sit next to his master. Sandy scratched the dog's ears. "Next flock, Jeff. We'll get some."

The rain gave way to a steady fall of oversized feathery snowflakes mixed with pelletlike granules that seemed closer to hail than snow. They touched the water and vanished. There was no malevolence in the snowfall, and it wasn't until his mustache began to ice up that the reality of just how cold it had become struck him. His hands and feet were feeling the chill, but his concern was mainly for Jeff—his spaniel's coat wasn't intended for extremes.

He heard the flock before he spotted it. Jeff looked straight up, but

Sandy resisted the temptation and kept his head down as the birds passed over. They circled out beyond the decoys, grumbling duckily among themselves—maybe a dozen birds altogether. He hunkered low, watching them just below the brim of his hat visor. Then, another collective whoosh of wings passed overhead. *More? All right!* Mixed in with the mallards of the second group was a very obvious drake pintail. They circled to the left, opposite the clockwise rotation of the first flock. *Be cool.*

Then, unexpectedly, a lone drake mallard glided in low and hovered for a moment over the decoys—nearly a replay of the first single he had missed. He shot the bird from a sitting position, then looked skyward, hoping for a chance at one of the circlers but knowing there would be none.

He sent Jeff for the bird, now floating among the decoys at the center of a ring of ripples. *Maybe I might have had a chance for more than one if I hadn't been so quick on the trigger. Still, a bird in the hand . . .* He got out of the boat to receive the mallard as Jeff pranced around with this first bird before delivering it. Sandy took the duck, then looked up in time to see a dozen ducks flaring away, back over the river. *The same bunch back for a second look? Maybe they got turned around in the snow—whatever, they're gone now. Damn.* The bird in his hand didn't seem quite the good investment it had a moment ago.

He dried the dog as best he could with a burlap. Jeff seemed impervious to the cold water, but Sandy knew better. The falling snow swirled in the gusts of wind, and watched it build up on the skim ice around the boat and on his decoys. After fifteen minutes, he was sure his decoys looked like snow-covered stumps from the vantage point of a flying duck, and he walked out to clear them. He dunked the eight nearest decoys, but the farther blocks were in deeper water, beyond the reach of his torn waders. They continued to look like floating igloos.

Wading back, he saw Jeff suddenly look up, then heard ducks above him. He crouched but quickly stood back up when he felt water rush in through the rip in his right leg. *Damn!* Overhead, the group of ducks split as it passed the point, with some following the river and others turning into the swamp. It was the flock with the pintail. While they hadn't responded to the decoys, they hadn't flared off as if they'd seen him do his scarecrow act, either.

He hurried back to the boat. Twice he heard ducks pass overhead, their wings hissing in the blowing snow. He willed them to swing over his decoys, but when he finally caught a glimpse of the flock, they seemed more intent on the shelter of the swamp behind him. After a long minute of waiting, he turned to look back just as a single was descending over the nearest treetops. He fired a quick shot, and as the bird tumbled, the rest of the flock erupted out of the swamp where they had all landed, unseen. They headed for the river, and in their confusion passed immediately in front of his boat. He singled out the pintail, but for once gave the too-close bird too much lead, then repeated his mistake with his third shot.

What a jerk! What an absolute JERK! I knew what I was doing wrong, yet still I pulled the trigger. He mocked his previous promise to himself, "If I can get just *one* shot, I'll be happy." He sat down in disgust, then noticed a drake mallard floating among the decoys. Its head was in the water. He could not say which of the missed shots at the pintail had caught the bird.

He sent Jeff to make the retrieve, then walked him back behind the boat to find the one he had taken with his first shot. Although they searched the snow-covered swamp thoroughly, Jeff showed no indication that he scented anything. At length, Sandy happened to take a hard look at what he had assumed was an old bird's nest in one of the swamp maples. When he shook the drake from the tree, Jeff pounced on it as if it had been discovered hiding.

Once Sandy sat back down, the cold began to gnaw at him. While he hadn't been toasty before, at least the chill had been tolerable. In duck hunting, keeping warm is a function of keeping dry, and now his right leg was wet. He grew colder with each passing minute. Snow needed to be cleared from his decoys once again, but his feet and legs were painfully cold and he had no ambition to go wading. He began to shiver.

Three ducks emerged from the snow. Like the previous flock, they too ignored his snow-covered decoys and banked toward the swamp. Two were blacks, with a drake mallard trailing behind. Sandy put the gun to his shoulder and pushed on the safety for what seemed a long time before it gave way under his numb finger. His first two shots were strangely quiet and echoless in the snow and only caused the trio to climb higher. He swung the gun as far as he could beyond his right shoulder and was actually falling backward when he touched off his third shot. The mallard folded, but seemed suspended for a long moment, growing steadily larger among the snowflakes until it finally fell heavily just a few feet from the boat.

He tried to reload, but his fingers were having trouble holding the shells. He recognized the signs.

"Let's go, Jeff."

He reflected that that might be the first intelligent decision he'd made all morning. The ice around the boat was substantial now, and he noticed the decoys were coated with ice. Using an oar, he quickly swept them into the boat. The result was a frozen tangle of anchor lines and weights. *To hell with it.* He was racing the cold now, and haste was imperative.

The motor would not turn over. He had left it tilted up rather than in the water, and now it was frozen like everything else. *Dumb ass. I should have known this would happen.* He laughed, but there was no humor in his voice. He had little feeling in his hands as he rigged the oarlocks and started down the river. It would be a long haul.

As he rowed, his frustration bothered him far more than the gnawing cold. He took too much pride in his wingshooting to excuse the morning with a shrug of the shoulders and a one-liner. Even the final overhead shot, as spectacular as it was, was only possible because he had screwed up on the initial two easy chances. He shook his head. *Some days you eat the bear. Other days, the bear eats you.* He rowed on, only slightly thankful that the labor warmed him.

He felt the boat rock a bit as Jeff leapt into the water. *What the hell. . . !* The dog was after a duck that could be seen slinking off along the undercut riverbank. After a short chase through the shallows, the springer caught the cripple, then stood waiting for his master to bring the boat to him. Sandy stood and rowed the boat to shore, grinning. Jeff, if nothing else, made every hunt interesting.

He dried off the dog, then wrapped him in the empty decoy sacks. The bird had shot wounds on the left side: There was no reason to doubt that it was the same drake mallard that had flown on after being hit an hour earlier.

Rowing again, he mused that this would be a day he remembered for his mistakes. His eyes kept returning to the five drake mallards now piled on the thwart. He grinned. There had certainly been plenty of duck hunts when everything went right—he stayed warm, all the equipment worked, and he remembered to bring all the things he should—but he still returned home empty-handed because no ducks flew. "Now *here's* an alternate ending for you, Jeff." He paused to rub the springer's head once more. "It just takes a bit of pretzel logic to recognize it."

Five birds! Sandy laughed out loud at the irony of it. He thought of an old Steeley Dan song that often popped into his head when things went awry. He never could recall the exact words: something about going crazy and laughing at the freezing rain. Even though the new verses he was making up didn't always rhyme, he sang out loud as he rowed in time to the song's rhythm through the snow.

Winter

HER BACK LEGS hurt. She sat on the floor of the truck in the early darkness, her head resting on the seat between the two men. Her master's hand idly scratched her ears as he drove and talked with the other man. She felt the stiffness in her muscles, but with each breath her whole being thrilled to the smells in her nostrils; both men wore jackets redolent with the odors of countless birds that had found their way into the game pockets, and her master's hands smelled of gun oil and the waterproofing he had used on his boots. She even liked the bitter smell of the coffee the men drank. She hardly noticed the ache. They were going hunting.

". . . and when I mentioned Buddy's Brit to him, all he wanted to know was how big the dog was—never mind if he's any damn good, just if he was *big*. The guy is out to breed giant Brittanies. What a chowderhead." Her master was speaking. He did most of the talking, usually. After eleven years with him, she had concluded that it was some form of communication between people, but she could never fathom the endless stream of words. She lay still, feeling his hand on her head and listening to his meaningless talk. Her eyes were half closed. She didn't know where they were heading, nor did she care. It was enough to know that they were going *hunting*. She was content.

When she felt the gravel road beneath the truck, she knew they were almost there. Not knowing why, she sat up. She waited for her master to say, "Take it easy, Suzie." The truck lurched around a corner. She whined impatiently.

"Take it easy, Suzie."

It was true, then. They were almost there.

She felt the truck slow, then stop, and then there was the always eerie silence when the engine was shut off. Both men opened their doors, but her master looked at her and said, "Stay." She listened to the sounds of the men outside, shivering as she forced herself to remain where she had been told. When she heard the tinkle of her own bell from outside, she could contain her excitement no longer and found herself at her master's feet. The other man laughed, and her master said, "I thought I told you to stay in the truck." But there was no sternness in his voice, so she sat smiling her open-mouthed dog's smile up at him. He slipped the bell onto her collar. "Now stay right here."

The men leaned against the truck, and the stream of talk continued. The sky grew brighter. She nosed along the edge of the field, smelling the mice and rabbits that had passed during the night. There was some days-old scent left by a male dog she didn't know. She smelled it closely.

The metallic sound of her master's gun closing brought her automatically to his side. The trembling started again.

"Is it time, Dad?"

"Close enough," the other man answered.

Her master pointed forward and softly whistled his "go ahead" signal. She charged into the short grass. Running, she crossed the breadth of the small field, doubled back, and saw him wave her ahead. She was propelled in these first minutes of the hunt by the pent-up excitement within her, and she knew only the pure joy of release. The music that was the sound of her bell filled her ears, and for the moment she felt neither the heavy frost underfoot nor the soreness in her legs. She kept running.

She made her turn at the field margin and was accelerating when she struck it. Her body spun around as she fought to stop against her forward momentum. The scent hung just above the frost: Mixed in with the poultry smell of feathers and the odor of dust and feces was the dark liquid scent of *fear*, and she sorted through the mixed multitude of signals in her nostrils to read that and that alone. She moved two steps closer, then a third before she sensed that the bird was in balance—trapped just enough so that it wouldn't run, yet not frightened enough to fly.

Behind her now she distantly heard the men's voices.

"Okay . . . You go ahead, Dad." Then, closer, her master's quiet tones. "Easy, girl . . . Steady now . . ."

As always, she was surprised when the bird took wing. It came out of the grass much farther away than she had thought it to be. There was a clatter of wings and a single shot, then the bird fell not far from where it had taken flight. Now, waiting for her command, she listened to the babble of talk around her:

"Good shot!"

"Naw . . . I should have let him get out farther."

"It looked pretty good from here."

"Hey, the old girl really did a good job on him. She jacked up like a champion."

"Yeah, that was nice. Good girl . . . Fetch dead, Suzabelle."

There it was. She went to the bird and carried it by its rump. The pheasant was dead, its odor fading and hardly discernible any longer over the strong, salty smell of blood. Her master was kneeling, and she was able to look into his eyes rather than up at the bottom of his chin.

"Good girl . . . Thank you." He rubbed her head as he took the bird from her. "Suzanna, you are one mighty fine bird dog." *Suzanna.* One in a long list of names she answered to, each with its own connotation; Suzabelle and Suzanna when she was being praised, Nit-Bit, Babe, and Suziski when they were having fun, and Bird-Brain when she had done something wrong. She couldn't understand names, and didn't try. The man with her master was "Dad," yet at home the children called her master by the same name.

He whistled her ahead again. Beyond the sumac at the field's edge she could smell water. The brook ran at the bottom of a little gully. She paused to wet her mouth, then leaped lightly to the other side. She could smell the fox before she climbed the far bank. He had passed an hour before, but his scent was strong. She loved the smell. For fifty feet she followed his tracks along the brook. She remembered a warm fall afternoon from years before when her master had stopped the truck and put her and her kennelmate into a cornfield. Instead of "bird," he had said "fox" over and over, using all the same words he used when they were looking for a cripple. When she saw the fox, she realized the scent she had so often found in the past didn't belong to another dog but to this small animal that outran her so effortlessly. Now she heard her master's whistle from across the brook, and without thinking, she turned and recrossed the gully, leaving the fox tracks and her memories on the other side.

Her pace gradually slowed to her normal trot. She was crossing the field, feeling the cold of the melting frost on her pads, when she heard the rumble of wings behind her. She looked back to see a pheasant in the air immediately in front of her master. *"Hen . . . Hen, Dad."* No shot was fired. For a reason she didn't understand, some pheasants were not taken. She watched the bird fly away.

"Suzie!" There was anger in his voice. In the scream of words that followed, the anger was all she heard. "What's the matter with you? The bird was right here." He pointed into the grass at his feet. She went to see where the bird had been because she knew he wanted her to, but she could never figure what was to be gained by it. There was

no scent in the air, and it wasn't until she actually stuck her nose beneath the matted weeds where the bird had roosted for the night that she found the pocket of scent.

"You walked right by her, Bird-Brain."

She looked at him. There were no two ways about it—that's where the bird had been. Is that what he wanted? He waved his arm in an underhand motion and said, "Okay now . . . Find 'em up." That one she knew. She turned and cast back into the field again.

Men couldn't smell. She had long suspected it, and that realization had changed the way she hunted. At the end of the field she smelled where two men and a dog had passed the same way just twenty minutes earlier, crossing into the cut-over corn beyond. She looked back, and her master waved her ahead into the same cornfield. Maybe he knew something she didn't.

They passed a fruitless half-hour in the stubble, following in the footsteps of the previous hunters. In her own way, she had known they would find nothing. At the end of the rows her master whistled her in. The other man sat on the fallen branch of a dead tree, and her master sat down beside him as she approached.

"Just a few minutes, Bill," the other man was saying. "I'm not the man I used to be. Hell, I'm not so sure I ever was."

Both men laughed. That was another thing that they did that she didn't understand. There had been a time when she had wondered about such things, but now she was just glad for a chance to lay at her master's feet and rest for a moment. They had been afield for two hours.

"Yeah, Suzie and I are getting old together . . ."

She looked up at the mention of her name but closed her eyes again when she realized the other man had not been talking to her.

"A dog's life is short no matter how you measure it," her master said. "But at least she's not going deaf, the way Duffy did near the end."

Duffy. The word caused an image of her old kennelmate to appear in her mind. She wondered where he had gone. For six years their lives had been intertwined, and she still emulated his technique for handling cripples, although she couldn't know she had originally learned the tactic from him. The last time she had seen him was nearly four years before, when her master had carried him a half-mile back to the truck.

"Starting a new puppy in the spring isn't something I'm really looking forward to, Dad."

"You don't figure you can get another year out of her?"

Her master shook his head. "She's on borrowed time now. Her legs are really shot. She'll be hobbling around by noontime."

"It's too bad. She's been a good one for you, Bill."

"That she has. . . ." He reached down and scratched her behind the ears as she lay at his feet. "It's too bad that puppies only come from breeding dogs—I'd sure like to clone this old girl."

Old Girl. She had lately come to realize that that had become another of her many names. She got to her feet when the men did. Her legs were stiff, and she walked gingerly until the tightness in her muscles eased. The men continued to talk as she trotted out into the next field. Her master's whistle called her back—they were turning to the left along the edge of the harvested corn. Her legs started to run in answer to his command, but she abruptly slowed to a trot when the pain stung her.

In the next field she worked the edge of the cut corn in front of the men, casting from the stubble into the brush at the field's edge. At the far turn of one cast she caught just a whiff of bird scent. She worked farther into the field, searching the air. Behind her, her master whistled to her: They were crossing through the brushline, heading down toward the river. Her legs responded, but there were birds out in the field somewhere behind her. She stopped in indecision. He whistled for her again. This time her legs only took a single step before she stopped them. She waited for him.

After a moment he came back out of the thick brush, looking for her. *"Suzie . . . This way."* He pointed behind him.

She stood still.

"Dad . . ." He turned and called back into the undergrowth. *"Out here . . . She's got birds."*

When she saw that both men were returning, she continued her search out into the stubble. The scent grew stronger, but it was scattered on the breeze across the open field. She worked the air, weaving back and forth, but she could isolate none of the several different scents being carried to her. Suddenly she recalled a situation from years before—she and Duffy were hunting stubble then, too. They had been unable to unravel the unclear combination of scents that became weaker when they tried to follow them. There had been many pheasants in the stubble that day, and those that had run out escaped in the confusion of scents. Remembering, she realized there must be several pheasants now running away from her toward the far brushline. She circled to the right, urging her sore legs to run.

She turned back into the field when she reached the brush along the edge. In the distance she saw her master and the other man crossing toward her. The birds had to be between them and her. The wind came over her tail as she cast through the rows, but she was certain the pheasants were here.

Fear. The scent hit her as abruptly as if she had run into a wire fence. She knew she was too close to the bird and dared not move.

"Point!" Her master's voice carried faintly across the distance. She heard the men coming, but she couldn't shift even her eyes. In front of her something shifted in the weeds. She didn't move.

The men drew closer, and the fear smell grew more intense. Then, the clatter of wings and the sound of voices: *"Hen. . . ! There's an-other. . . ! And a third one. . . !"* No shots were fired. *"Hold up, Dad. She's got a whole flock corralled—there's got to be a rooster in here somewhere."* She couldn't move. The scent in her nostrils was stronger than ever.

The men moved closer to her, then stopped, and for a long moment there was utter silence. Then suddenly the pheasant was in the air, springing straight up in an extravaganza of color and flailing wings, screaming a call she sometimes heard in her sleep. Still crowing, the bird leveled off and started into the wind, then turned toward the brushline, picking up speed. She heard the gun's report. The pheasant faltered and fell into the blackberry bushes at the field's edge.

"Go fetch, Suzie." There was excitement in her master's voice. She started off but found her legs would not run. She and thorns had never been on the best of terms, and she picked her way through, crawling on her belly as she followed the strong smell of the crippled bird. The pheasant retreated from her to the far edge of the thicket but now could go no farther and crouched facing her, hackles raised. She pawed at it, then snapped quickly when the cock struck at her foot, flipping the bird over to grab it by the back. It was Duffy's old trick. The pheasant's spurs slashed harmlessly away from her. When she squeezed the bird to stop its struggling, one of its wings covered her eyes. The sound of her master's whistle guided her back to him, but the briars were difficult enough even when she could see them, and it seemed she had traveled much farther than she should have.

She emerged from the blackberries. Close by she heard the other man shout, *"Here she is, Bill."*

"Fetch him here, Suzie." Her master's voice came from far away. She started toward the sound with the bird held high.

"Good girl," he said as he took the pheasant from her. Then, as he sometimes did when he was especially pleased, he lifted her in his arms.

The other man reached out and scratched her head. "That's the best piece of bird work I've ever seen," he said. "Ever."

"Bird sense," her master stated. "You've heard me say it a hundred times, Dad—any dog can smell a bird, but bird sense makes bird dogs. And you, Suzabelle, are one mightly fine bird dog, aren't 'cha, Babe." He reached to pet her, but as he did, her weight shifted in his arms, and he squeezed her slightly. She yelped in pain. He eased her back to the ground.

The other man shook his head.

They retraced their steps and crossed through the brushline into the next field. It was still early in the day, and although they were hunting familiar ground, she couldn't recall this place being so taxing. She was tired. The pain in her legs seemed worse. There was a giant oak tree in the center of the field they were hunting. Several seasons before she had found a pheasant beneath that tree, but today it seemed just too far away.

She slowed to a walk as the morning waned toward noon. Her master urged her ahead, but fatigue dragged on her. They rested again, this time by the edge of the river. She waded in the murky water and for a little while felt refreshed. It didn't last. They hunted into some familiar overgrown asparagus beds where they had often found birds in the past. She recalled a time when she would race through this thick stuff all day, but today she couldn't imagine how. She was quite suddenly exhausted and knew that if she could just sit down for a while she'd be full of energy once again and would work this asparagus like she knew she should.

When her bell stopped, he waved to the other man, and they approached with guns at port arms. She was sitting in a small opening in the cover, looking back at him with what he imagined to be apology in her eyes. He handed his gun to the other man and lifted her again in his arms. He didn't speak but turned and started back toward where the truck was parked.

Cradled against her master's chest, she breathed in the wonderful smells of his canvas hunting coat; bird stench, gunpowder, and the strong scent of him. She could feel his breathing as he carried her. She thought again of Duffy and the last time she had seen him. Her legs hurt, but with her master, as always, she knew that soon things would be better. She closed her eyes.

...and Fishing, Too

THERE'S A PLACE in central Massachusetts where the state built a dam
fifty years ago and flooded out a bunch of little towns to provide a
water supply for the city of Boston. They took over all the surrounding
land that made up the reservoir's watershed, too. In the years since,
the area has come to represent a wilderness preserve where *everything*
isn't allowed. (The signs read, "No hunting, trapping, camping, hik-
ing, picnicking, or trespassing." It's always fun to stop and read them,
because no one can resist the temptation to invent new forbidden
items: "It says, 'No hunting, fishing, camping, bird watching, tree
climbing, teeth picking, leak taking . . .'") The only way an ordinary
citizen can get into the place is via the one thing they do allow . . . you
can fish on the main body of water.

Ah, but the fishing is what Quabbin is all about.

Fishermen from miles around line up at the three access gates
before dawn each morning, trailered boats in tow, and the overheard
conversations in the dark stillness are invariably of rigs and baits and
depths and water temperatures and, of course, the fish: lake trout and
rainbows and walleyes and largemouth bass. For those who live in the
western part of the state, Quabbin reservoir is to fishing what Uncle
Josh is to pork rinds: It's a standard of excellence, maybe not *the* one
best, but certainly everybody's idea of top drawer. It is the most heavily fished body of water in Massachusetts. (The swan boat pond on
Boston Common is the only possible exception.) There aren't any
sailboats or water-skiers or racing boats—they're not allowed. You can
take a canoe to see the scenery, but the place is so big, and the fact that
you are forbidden from stepping ashore makes the place less than
"sightseer-friendly." Quabbin is for *fishing,* and whether the fishing is
any better or worse than other places is something I'll leave to those
for whom that sort of argument is important. It's enough to say that
for years Quabbin was what fishing was all about for my Dad.

When I was a kid, I thought so too.

There are still a few heavy-duty terms that can bring back the bone-chilling dawns of trolling while the outboard vibrated my fillings and my brain loose—terms like *lead-core line* and *Davis spinner* and *laker*, and one that seems innocent enough but still socks me every time: *shiner bucket*. My father was enamored with terms too, but for him the terms were *walleye* and *rainbow* and *big-laker* (one word). The accepted way of catching walleyes and rainbows and big-lakers was by trolling, so we trolled. Now, I want you to understand that I've got nothing against trolling or people who troll, but when you're a seven-year-old kid, it's just not the sort of thing to keep your attention for very long. Eventually one or the other of my brothers and I would end up punching each other. My father would shut off the motor and say, "All right, youze kids don't wanna fish no more, pick up an oar . . . the both of youze . . . now start oaring."

You can't get very far away from an angry father in a twelve-foot boat, and Dad could use his fishing rod like a buggy whip to get your attention. So we'd oar. Dad would get out his casting rod and work the shoreline while we sullenly rowed, certain that we were abused children. Once I recall he hooked one while I was doing galley slave duty. He was using a yellow plug called a Van Spook that was a little smaller than a three-cell flashlight. We nearly tipped the boat over trying to see what had taken his lure, but when the fish showed himself, I felt like the guys in the cartoons when the whale surfaces under their boat: This was something *big*.

When Dad finally netted the thing and brought it aboard, it turned out to be a monster of a three-foot pickerel. They're usually sleazy sort of fish, hanging out in the weeds and lily pads, but this one was caught in deep water off a rocky ledge. I was barely three feet long myself then, so it seemed all the bigger—a prehistoric-looking thing, with more teeth than my whole family, including the dogs. I couldn't find a place in the boat far enough away from that fish. It was several more years before I let myself trail my hand in the water again as we trolled. I kept imagining that mouthful of teeth just below the surface. In the more boring moments I stuck to fooling around with the minnows in the shiner bucket.

Or, I'd investigate my father's tackle box.

Compared to Dad's old green metal "fishin' box," the plastic affairs they sell today are cheap imitations. It was as big as a steamer trunk (well, maybe a medium-sized two-suiter) and not only had two triple rows of accordion-hinged drawers, but was as full of nooks and crannies as any roll-top desk. It held a fascinating array of tackle, tools, and genuine junk in which someone more erudite than I might have read a history of the fisherman who was my father. There were some lures that must have been one-of-a-kind items. Dad had a silver spoon in there with three red plastic jewels set into it—it was bigger than most of the fish we caught. He had rubber frogs and old jars with pork rinds, and there was a nifty hair bass bug that looked like a mouse. He never let me use it. (I've got it in my tackle box now, and my kids are as fascinated by it as I was.) But it wasn't just fishing stuff in there: There were things like odd-shaped pliers and patch kits, and I remember he kept a big magnet for some reason I never fully understood. Old pieces of newspaper from before I was born lined the drawers and compartments. Rummaging around in there was like digging through some interesting person's attic.

"Hey, Dad—did you ever catch anything on this?"

"Naw. That's a lure Bobby Pumpquist left in the boat one time. Put it back before you hook yourself on it."

"Last time I asked you, you said you caught a muskie on it once at Lake Champlain when you were with Kid Louie."

"That was last time. Now put it back."

QUABBIN WAS a wonderful place to be a kid, especially a kid from the suburbs who had more than just a passing interest in the outdoor stories in *Boys' Life*. When the state wanted to reintroduce wild turkeys, Quabbin, an honest-to-goodness wilderness area, was the logical place to start. There were nearly always deer to be seen, and the ever-fascinating poetry of barn swallows in flight. There were herons in the shallows and mergansers with their young and families of Canada geese and turtles when the sun chased the chill off the water. And eagles. Being a certifiable wilderness, Quabbin was and still is home to several pairs of bald eagles. Not many, but everyone that goes there is sure they see one—of course, nobody ever sees a red-tailed hawk or a vulture at Quabbin. If it soars, it *has* to be an eagle.

The place itself is an endless source of amazement: There are coves and inlets and passes that lead to other coves and inlets, and several open bodies of water whose dimensions are measured in miles. There are old roads that run into the water and then back out again, and in some places where the pavement hasn't given out below, a boater can follow the road's clear path into the middle of a weed bed. Stone walls cling to hillsides in what were once pastures but have since been flooded over. Follow a wall where it goes into the water, and if you look over in the right place, you can see it below the boat, ten feet down. There are rock ledges that were once sheer hillside cliffs, and deep water where rivers flowed in valleys not so long ago. A few years back, using a topo map that only showed the water surface and none of the flooded terrain, we navigated to the deepest spot using the map markings for the present day town boundaries: the boundaries are the old rivercourses. My father was a nonbeliever until he saw an extra thirty feet of dry anchor line go over. The two lakers I pulled up that day remain the biggest fish I've ever caught in fresh water.

When I was a kid, the biggest outboard allowed on Quabbin was ten horsepower. As a result, there was a constant market for old motor cowlings that said Johnson 9½ or Evinrude 10 on them. People would somehow fit these old covers over the big motors that were needed if they were to get where they wanted to be on the big water without spending all morning getting there. Dad had a 5½, but boats would fly by us doing forty knots, planing along and hardly leaving any wake, and everyone wondered how they managed to go that fast with that old beat-up Merc. The fact that the motor had eight spark plug wires sticking out of it never seemed to matter, 'cause it said ten horsepower plain as day right on the side.

DAD HAD A BUNCH of fishing buddies back then; Joe Metnick and Herb Beeler and Uncle Hank and Girard Ford, but the most memorable was a man who worked in the shop with Dad named Walt Stewart. He had several grown-up children of his own, and in retrospect, he had an inordinate amount of patience with his fishing partner's sons. After many investigations, I concluded that his tackle box wasn't equal to my Dad's, but it finished a close second: In there, among other things, he had a small folding gaff. At times, against the chill, my Dad and Mr. Stewart would bring along a jug—nothing serious, just something to keep the fluids flowing. On the particular early spring day I recall, the evaporation rate must have been fairly high, because even a little kid like me could see how quickly the level in the bottle of Southern Comfort was receding. And, looking back, I realize it *was* cold: The mists hung low and thick, and the surface of the water was like oil. Mr. Stewart was changing lures, tying on a Flatfish of a size designed to catch medium-sized tuna. (In a story like this a writer can only mention a lure by name if he has something good to say about it. So let me state here that I've always thought Flatfish really *looked* good, even though I've never actually known anyone who has caught any-thing on one. But every tackle box has several. I especially like the ones that have two pairs of treble hooks on little extension wires—I guess that someone really thought that someday a second fish might want to hit that lure while a first was being reeled in and all those extra hooks might come in handy.) After adjusting his glasses several times, Mr. Stewart finished tying the elaborate knot and set the big Flatfish on the boat seat next to him while he reeled in the slack in his line and cast out toward the ledge we were following. He assured me that the special knot was needed for the lunker he was about to catch. I guess he thought it was about time he tried out his gaff after all those years of carrying it in his box. Then I noticed that the Flatfish was still on the boat seat and called Mr. Stewart's attention to that minor fact, with all the subtlety you'd expect from any nine-year-old boy. After a moment's consideration, he threw the Southern Comfort bottle toward the shoreline, closed his tackle box, and sat with crossed arms for the remainder of the morning while my father unsuccessfully tried to stifle his laughter.

I ALMOST CAUGHT a big rainbow there one time. From the time I was ten up until I was thirteen or so, my father went through his walleye period. The state was releasing thousands of walleyes in Quabbin in an attempt to establish that species there, and my Dad read everything he could find about them and bought special rigs for them and fished almost exclusively for them. To the best of my knowledge the total number of walleyes he caught at Quabbin was zero. On this particular day, after another fruitless morning of trolling for them, Dad was bottom fishing for walleyes in a deep cove. I was bored silly and put on a bobber and a glob of nightcrawlers. The odds of catching a monster trout on such a less-than-subtle rig are about the same as getting hit by a meteorite on Groundhog Day, but it happened. As luck would have it, I still had a twenty-pound test leader on the end of my trolling rig, having been too unconcerned to change it off, so I was able to horse that lunker right up next to the boat in about as much time as it takes to tell about it. If I had played the fish and allowed him to tire himself out, Dad might have been able to net him, but try telling that to an eleven-year-old kid who can already see himself pictured on the outdoor page of the *Springfield Union*, holding a fish so big that his arms are sagging. *How big?* Well, how big a fish would it take to impress you? Would you believe me if I said that on four or five tries, Dad couldn't get him into the big long-handled boat net? *I didn't think so.* The trout was fighting so hard that he would slam the net away each time Dad went to scoop him up, and he was too big to fit in sideways. After a few seconds the line parted. End of fish story. But to this day, whenever I tell someone about that incident I feel like the guy who really *did* leave his wallet in his other pants: Fishermen have a reputation for stretching the truth, but in this case only the exaggerations are true.

WHEN I STARTED writing about Quabbin, I vowed I'd stay away from statistics on how big the place is and how many fish are caught there and the like—nobody cares, anyway. But there are some stats that I can't keep out of the story: From 1951 to the present the total number of things lost in the water and the surrounding bushes at Quabbin by people whose last name is the same as mine comes to:

    724 lures and spinners
    207 hook-line-and-sinker rigs
 1,441 yards of assorted fishing line
     18 bottles and cans of beverage placed in water for cooling and believed to have been stolen by mischievous fish
      8 pairs of sunglasses
      1 entire rod and reel (see below list of "really big ones hooked but not landed")
      2 sneakers (actually, it was just one. The other one was thrown in as a reply to my brother's question of, "Well, dummy, what are you going to do now with just one sneaker?")

During the same period, we collectively drowned

 2,008 nightcrawlers
   339 garden variety worms (Obviously, nightcrawlers were always the "bait of preference.")
   981 martyred shiners (311 unused shiners released on their personal recognizance)

while getting a grand total of

 4,322 nibbles
   297 fish hooked but not landed
   362 "really big ones" hooked but not landed (includes all of the above 297 plus 65 inanimate and unyielding objects hooked on the bottom while trolling)
   141 pounds of aquatic vegetation
     3 turtles

I LIKE TO TAKE my daughters to Quabbin. They seem to see the same things there that I look for, maybe because fishing is something we do incidental to a day on the water. We bring binoculars and a picnic lunch and suntan lotion as well as our fishing rigs. Both daughters can cast a mean bass plug now, but, like me, they haven't lost touch with the idea that since we're just fooling around, an eight-inch bluegill is as much fun as a three-pound bass. Fish only arrange themselves on a totem pole of descending importance in the eyes of serious fishermen, or those who'd like to be serious fishermen. It wasn't so long ago that I had my hands full keeping their hooks baited while they caught pumpkinseeds.

"Daddy, my bobber sunk."

"You've got a fish on—reel in."

She'd crank the handle on the all-plastic Zebco rig until the little bluegill was eyeball-to-eye with the end of the rod. "What do I do now, Daddy?"

Fishing's fun. But the turtles are as much a part of Quabbin for them as the fish are, and the swallows and kingfishers and the deer that stand and look curiously out at the boat. And, of course, the eagles. But they see too that Quabbin represents a world that doesn't know or care about their world of teenage fashions and diet Pepsi and MTV. And I hope they know which of the two is the more important.

THERE ARE COUNTLESS other impoundments around the country, places where other fathers take their children to catch fish and marvel at a wilderness where the waters are unlittered by nonreturnable bottles and styrofoam cups and the vistas contain only the hills and the sky. For a nonfishing fisherman, going to a place like Quabbin becomes a manifestation of a primordial urge: It's the same urge that causes him to hang prints of Francis Golden's watercolors in his office and to turn down the heat in his home and build a log fire on the hearth. It's sometimes difficult for him to remember that man and his doings make up an artificial world, and that underneath the asphalt and concrete the real world is still there, sustaining and growing and renewing itself. And that he too, for all his arrogance and worldliness, is just another of Nature's many children. Quabbin is there, because sometimes a man has to go see for himself.

Wisdom

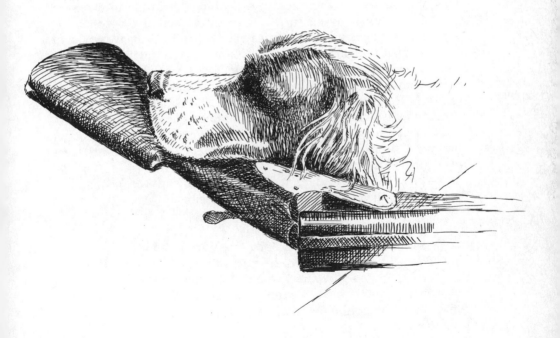

This is kinda like fishing: Sometimes you just get a nibble, but no fish.

—Brennan Roy, age eleven, watching
my dog false point while working
pheasants

THE IDEA that I needed a new puppy struck me when I counted years on my fingers and discovered that Win had been five on her last birthday. My first dog, Duffy, had spent his life with my parents for any number of reasons, but mostly because I didn't have the heart to take him away from my mother when I got married and moved out. So although I had owned bird dogs for twelve years, the joy of having two dogs digging up the back yard at the same time had never been mine.

A new puppy was definitely in my future, but I was curious as to what I was letting myself in for. Each advantage of a second dog seemed to be offset by one of a series of drawbacks. There were a lot of field trial men I might have talked to, some of them with more dogs than Carter has peanuts. Unfortunately, to a man they violently disagreed with my keeping bird dogs in the house rather than outside in a kennel. That's what made Tom's advice particularly valuable. He had been living with any number of bird dogs sleeping on and under his porch for years. His yard looked like an artillery practice range, and the most vile words in his wife's vocabulary were "dog hair." Here was the man I needed to talk to.

We were paired as judges at a little field trial and were cooling our heels between heats. I didn't beat around the bush.

"Tom, what about two dogs?"

"I've got more 'n that."

"Yeah, I know. I'm thinking of buying a second dog. . . ."

"Okay. Gimme a hundred an' you can take home my Pete dog there." He indicated a hyperactive pointer puppy, just completing his millionth lap around his three-foot chain stake. "Matterafac', I'll even come out an' shoot him for you in a month or so when you can't take him no more."

"No, no. I don't want to buy one of *your* dogs, for Chrissake. I want some of your advice."

"Don't buy a pointer." Tom shook his head.

"I won't. But what do you think of the theory that two dogs will keep each other entertained? I've heard that you don't have as much of a problem with them digging and trying to get out of the yard and such."

"You can't never tell." Tom scratched the stubble on his chin. "Sometimes, a couple of bored dogs'll spell each other diggin' under the fence. Guess they figure it's faster that way, an' they ain't as tired when they finally tunnel out." He grinned at me. "Really, though, sometimes a pup'll make an old dog young again. But sometimes, too, an old mutt will decide he's gonna rule the roost and won't have nothin' to do with the pup 'cept to bite him once in a while, and there goes your companionship idea." He added, "The only real answer for that is to be sure that the pup you buy is gonna grow bigger than the dog you've got now."

"I don't know if I like that idea." An image had appeared in my imagination. "Fifteen years and three dogs from now, I'll have a bird dog I can put a saddle on and ride around like a horse."

Tom shrugged. "That's fair."

I consulted the next item on my mental checklist. "How about one dog helping to train the other? They say the only thing a pup learns from an older dog is bad habits."

"'They say, They say . . .' Who's this '*They*' that keeps tellin' you all this stuff?"

"All the dogs I've ever talked to."

There was a long pause. "That explains a lot about you, Mulak." We both grinned. "It can go either way, that trainin' thing. Sometimes a dog'll help you out by settin' a good example. And competition between a pup an' an older dog can be useful if you handle it right." Tom leaned back on his flimsy folding chair and lit a Lucky. "On the other hand, try as I might, the only thing my Jill dog there ever learned from ol' Mike was t' lift her leg. She never did that before I owned her." As if on cue, Jill irrigated her stake in the manner of a male dog.

I persisted. "How about jealousy? Two dogs under the same roof as pets . . . The kids are bound to favor one over the other. How do you handle that?"

"That's pretty much the same as the others: You can't never tell ahead of time. Dogs're all individuals—some will an' some won't." He shrugged. "Hell, sometimes *I'm* jealous of *my* dogs. . . ."

"You're not much help, you know that?" I put on a bit of mock exasperation. "Here I've come all this way . . ."

"All the way from Chicopee . . ." Tom prompted.

". . . from Chicopee to sit at the feet of the dog guru and listen to his advice, and instead of wisdom all I've gotten is a pantsload of maybe's."

For a moment Tom screwed up his face in thought, then smiled when he had just the right response. "Okay—but you gotta promise to keep this a secret. When you're dealing with mutts, the only thing that's sure 'bout gettin' a second dog . . ." He leaned close and whispered. ". . . is that you'll have twice as much dog shit to pick up. Guaranteed. None of that other stuff you've heard is true . . . necessarily. There: You wanted wisdom, you got it." He pointed his finger in my face. "Now then, my advice don't come cheap: *One beer*. You buy."

I bought.

The Poacher

AT THIS TIME of the morning Russell always thought the garage looked like a drawing by Andrew Wyeth, with sunbeams through the dirty south-facing window cutting obtuse angles with the floor. If he allowed his eyes to focus on something illuminated within the square puddles of light, the rest of the interior blacked out and he couldn't really see that instead of rustic tin buckets and scythes the walls inside his garage were hung with garden hoses and snow shovels. He stood for a moment, a leather dog collar in his hand, sure of what he needed to do but reluctant to pass the point in time that would make accomplished fact of his intention. There was a bell attached to the collar, and for a moment the vibrato of its last ring was the only sound in the dark silence. At length he shook his head and, cursing himself under his breath, deliberately hung the collar on a nail driven into one of the joists. Then he turned and walked out of the Wyeth drawing into the sunlight.

CARS CONTINUALLY passed him as he drove on the highway. There were times, particularly in idle moments like these, when he debated the right and wrong of what he was doing. "If taking game ever gets so important to me that I've got to start breaking the law, I'll take up bank robbery or something where law-breaking really pays some dividends." He recalled saying that not so long ago. His Brittany sat on the floor of the passenger's side, her head on the seat. He reached down and scratched Pearl behind her ears. Brittanies had gotten their start as poachers' dogs in France. Russell smiled to himself, thinking this one was going to get another chance at it. Another car passed him, doing sixty-five.

He drove by the orchard and the chalkboard sign ("Macs—1/2 bu $3.00"), then slowed and took a left a quarter-mile farther along. As his truck bounced along the gravel road, Pearl sat up, muttering nervously: She recognized the indications that they were almost there. On his left, brand new paper signs were tacked to the run-down fence bordering the road. They promised all trespassers prosecution to the fullest extent of the law. The line where the landowner was supposed to sign his name was left blank.

Russell drove across a little swampy creek and followed the road up the other side, going slowly so as not to miss the turn-off. A few hundred yards farther, hardly noticeable in the thick laurel, was a house trailer, long since abandoned. He eased his truck into the drive and pulled up next to the old hulk. Standing at his truck, he could see the road, but only if he looked straight back along the drive. No one was going to notice that he'd parked here—at least, so long as they weren't intentionally looking for him. He stuffed his hunter orange hat under the seat, and put on the brown Jones cap he used for duck hunting. Today he'd rather not be noticed.

Downhill was a beaver dam where he could cross the brook. Coming onto the posted land this way from off the road, he had crossed none of the "no trespassing" signs. That didn't make it any more right, but at least he wasn't being blatant about it. He laughed under his breath at his attempt at self-delusion.

This was the cover he knew as "Mister John's." Behind the active orchard along the main road was an extensive series of forgotten fields and wooded margins—perfect bird cover, bordered by a swamp on one side and a dairy farm on the other. Years before, when he had stopped at the same roadside apple stand he had passed today, the old man he spoke to had initially said no to his request for permission to hunt. Before giving up, Russell had tried one last tack: "If it's a matter of you not wanting to have the birds on your property hunted, that's fine—I'll go. But if you're wondering if I'm the sort of person who shoots out barn windows or cuts fences or steals apples, let me assure you that I'm not." That had earned him a nod, and soon afterward he was hunting. When he presented Mister John with the native rooster he had taken that day, he made a friend. "I used to hunt these dragons myself," Mister John had said. "Always had a lot of respect for 'em. I gave it up when my eyesight started to go: Couldn't hit 'em clean any more—too many cripples runnin' off for fox bait."

Russell had opened the season here last week, but unlike previous opening days, he hadn't gotten the chance to offer his first bird to Mister John. As he crossed the beaver dam, he thought back to that morning:

> Any year's first pheasant was always cause for a minor celebration, and Russell was still wearing his self-congratulatory grin when a voice from the opposite side of the fence row called to him.

"Hey, you—unload your gun."

He did, even though he didn't have to be told to open his gun when someone else was around. "Hello. I didn't see you there."

The stranger had a .22 pumpgun tucked under his arm and a hunting license pinned to his cap, but he obviously wasn't hunting: He wore a pair of loafers. "Is that your truck parked in the barway?"

"What's the problem?" Russell had left his truck where he always parked.

"Didn't you see the signs? This is my sister's land, and she don't want nobody hunting here."

The stranger's dirty blue cap proclaimed that he was a fan of Ford farm equipment. Russell wondered if Ford wouldn't want their hat back. "I've hunted here for years, and have always talked to John down at the farm stand. As far as I know, this is his land and it's okay for me to hunt here." He regretted never having learned Mister John's last name.

Blue Hat stepped closer to him. "I'm telling you to get out."

Russell abandoned any pretension of politeness. "Yeah? Well I'm telling *you*, fella', that you're all wet. I'm hunting here with full permission of the landowner. . . ."

"John died last Christmas. My sister owns this now, and she don't want nobody hunting here."

A silence hung in the air for a long moment. So Mister John was dead. Russell felt sorrow and anger at the same time. And defeat. He whistled to Pearl and started along the field edge back toward his truck. Blue Hat walked immediately behind him. At length Russell said, "You can unload your gun any time—I'm leaving."

"Not until I see you drive off. I've copied down your license tag number, so don't try comin' back."

"Are you always this ornery, or is this just a front?"

"A few years back, somebody shot out my sister's back window . . ."

Russell stopped and turned to the man. "And you think it was me, right?"

"No, I'm not sayin' that . . ."

"Well, that's the way it sounds to me."

"She don't want nobody huntin' here . . ."

"Hold it." Russell raised his hand. "Answer me—if you don't think it was me who did the shooting, why are you out here with a loaded rifle? It's not like I'm stealing a bushel of your topsoil.

I've hunted this land for a dozen years or so—Mister John never had reason to complain, but all of a sudden I'm a criminal."

"It's not just you—she don't want nobody here."

"So you've said." Russell's sarcasm went unnoticed. "Watch out, though—the next guy you run off might not feature you coming after him with a loaded rifle. There's something in the law about that—assault, I think they call it." He turned in disgust and walked away, knowing he had said too much to a man who didn't have the brains of a two-dollar dog. Maybe at one time someone had fired a gun too close to a house. Maybe. The land hadn't been posted, after all, and not everyone went through the formality of asking permission. But he was certain that no one had shot out a window. Those things didn't happen in reality. He shook his head. And Mister John was no more. That was something that really was too bad.

THE BACK-UP behind the new beaver dam could not yet be termed a pond: It was simply an irregular area that had been flooded, leaving alders and streamside birches standing knee-deep in the water. As proof that the flood was no accident, canals led to still-dry areas where pointed stumps were surrounded by wreaths of woodchips on the ground. Some seemed fresh enough to have been gnawed the night before.

Pearl pointed. In these alders it had to be a woodcock. He approached from her flank, and when the bird bounced up and twittered off, he knelt and called his dog to him. There was no way to explain to her that today some shots were going to be passed up, but he petted her and scratched her ears.

They followed a woodline up into a series of abandoned pastures. The absence of the dog's bell was disquieting. His Brittany seemed such an extension of Russell's will that his occasional quiet whistle to her was all but unnecessary, but he hadn't realized how much he relied on the sound of the bell to track her. At one point their course took them close to the electric fence of a dairy farm's pasture, guarded as always by a line of bright orange 'no trespassing' signs. Russell had never been able to gain permission to hunt the farm's cornfields. Several Holsteins watched them vacantly until they had passed out of sight again.

There were years of memories in this place. He was smiling to himself, remembering a time when his dad had been with him, and they had each taken one of the pair of roosters Pearl's predecessor had found beneath a stunted thornapple. It had been right along in these blueberries somewhere . . . He hadn't been paying attention, and when he looked up, his Brit was standing on point by the same apple tree, in a near-perfect imitation of the scene in his memory. He smiled. *Who's going to believe this?* he thought. Pearl had the bird pinned, and Russell had to literally kick it up. As the pheasant leveled off, its tail flipped from vertical to horizontal. Russell chose that instant to shoot the bird in the head.

There followed a moment when, in another time, he would have stopped to field-dress the pheasant and spend a moment digesting the glow of a job done correctly. Instead he took the bird from Pearl and hurried downhill, out of the overgrown field and into the wood edge across the brook. When he thought he had traveled far enough so as not to be associated with the gunshot, he found a tree stump and sat to clean the bird.

The moment wasn't the same: Though he was out of breath, it was for the wrong reason. Guilt shouldn't be a part of successes, but it shared his seat now.

His wife shook the water from the pheasant and placed the naked bird on a square of freezer paper. Russell wrapped and taped the package.

"I can never understand it." He spoke more to himself than to his wife. "What do people think they're accomplishing by posting open land? I could see if the guy lived on the land, or was using it for something. But why post *open* land? Does the guy think a sign's going to stop the sort of people who steal cordwood or are careless with fire?" With a wax crayon he marked "10/29—Mr. John" on the wrapped package. "It's crazy," he said as he crossed the kitchen to the freezer. "The only people a guy like that ends up keeping out are law abiders—people he'd probably welcome in the first place."

His wife had heard it all before. Many times. "Isn't there something the club can do? Maybe there's somebody you can talk to?"

Two years before Russell had joined a sportsmen's club. At first it seemed a good place to air his ideas and frustrations, since the organization professed to be devoted to the preservation of open lands. The increase in the amount of posted land was a problem evident to anyone who knew enough to be concerned. But he soon found the club to be more interested in its own internal workings than any altruistic cause. He had joined ranks with fund-raisers, parliamentarians, and social meeting-goers. He laughed in disgust. "That bunch? Come on."

His wife dried her hands and hung the towel on the handle of the oven door. "Which one did you lose?"

"Mister John's. He died. Now his sister's got the whole place posted."

She looked at him for a long moment. She knew where he had hunted that day. "It's not like you go hunt posted land."

"I know," he said. "There's really no good explanation for it. You've heard me grouch about lost covers before, but Mister John's was something special. I'm having a hard time with the idea that I'm not supposed to go back—there's a lot of memories there."

She was slow to reply. "I don't like what's going on, Russ. You're making excuses for yourself, and that's not like you, either."

Later he sat with her, staring into the cherry wood fire on the hearth. "Think of an old man, one who's outlived his friends and discovers that his memories are populated by dead folks. That's how I'm beginning to feel. So many of my hunting memories are of places that are housing projects or shopping centers now." He shook his head. "That sort of thing is inevitable. This is different: Someone's perverted sense of entitlement is trying to keep me off of a place I've loved for years."

She took a breath as if to say something, but then changed her mind. There was an absence of dialogue that lasted for several minutes. At length, as if reading her thoughts, he said, "Trespassing is a felony. A difficult one to prove, to be sure, but a felony nonetheless. And I've been told once to stay out."

"Remember what you've often told me," she said. "More than anything else, wisdom is caution."

He mulled over her sentiments for a moment. He nodded but made no reply.

HE SPENT a Saturday hunting with Chem Romuluski. Chem was the best shot he knew. Probably the most amazing thing about his shooting was that he did it with a Remington 870 right out of the box—a perfectly ordinary gun in the hands of an extraordinary wingshot. But Chem was a poacher. He spoke freely of "hunting posted," and Russell found himself out of sympathy with some of Chem's equivocations: "I hunted that Audubon place way back before those nature fakers took it over. They've got to catch me to prove anything, and as long as I've got a gun, they ain't gonna catch me."

Measuring his own actions against Chem's, he saw how obviously self-righteousness clouded judgment. Although he wished he could be as sure of any one thing as Chem seemed to be about everything, he came away with his own actions in clearer focus.

HE HAD BEEN CAUGHT picking up litter. A farm truck stopped as he was emptying his gamebag of several bottles and soda cans.

"What're you doin'?" A weathered face looked out of the truck.

"I was hunting that swamp edge over there." Russell pointed across to the far side of the road.

"No—I mean with them bottles?"

"Oh, this is just some trash that was along the road."

"Is it worth anything?"

Russell smiled. "No. It's just junk."

"Why'd you pick it up, then?"

"Because the road looked better without it."

The face looked at him for an uncomfortably long time without saying anything. Finally the man muttered, "You people come out here and throw that trash around, stands to reason you ought to pick it up."

Russell watched the truck drive off, then poured some water into the plastic cover of a shell box for Pearl. "*You people,*'" he muttered. As if every stranger is a slob. He shook his head. A leaf fluttered into the water dish, and he bent to pick it out. He had parked beneath a huge spreading oak, now nearly naked late in November. The tree had grown in the open for a hundred years or more, and its branches reached outward rather than upward as a forest tree's might. He had compared enough leaves to know that even though every oak leaf looks like every other oak leaf, no two were identical. He studied the leaf as he leaned against his truck. "'You people.'" It was a convenient assumption. Too bad people can't be categorized that easily. They tend to be what they prove themselves to be—irresponsible idiots, thugs, slobs, and sometimes even sportsmen. You can't tell at a glance; they all *look* like hunters. He laughed out loud, but there was no humor in his laugh.

Pearl looked up for a moment before returning her attention to the water dish. He stood listening to his own thoughts for a moment. "Next week we'll give Mister John's one last visit, Pearl. What do you think?" The Brit wagged her stub tail and looked at her master, aware only that he was talking to her.

LATE IN THE AFTERNOON he parked next to the gutted house trailer in the laurel thicket. It had just started to snow, and his tire tracks hardly showed in the sugaring on the fallen leaves. Russell took a pair of low brass shells from his pocket and slid them into his gun. Hunters everywhere would certainly have a lot less trouble if their guns went "plink" rather than "ka-BOOM," he reflected.

The beaver pond was still open, and a single black duck flushed into the falling snow as Russell stepped onto the dam. An hour later the snow turned to sleetlike pellets as he and Pearl hunted through the low blueberry bushes behind the dairy farm. This was the last Saturday of hunting for Russell. Next week the deer season began. He looked at the clean imprint left by his vibram soles. *The deer hunters will be grateful for this snow*, he thought.

Pearl crossed under the row of orange signs and cast into a harvested cornfield. The harvester had taken only the corn, and the field was littered with naked corncobs among the knocked-down stalks. A flock of crows took flight at Pearl's approach, complaining noisily. Beyond them, a hundred yards away at the edge of the field, a hen pheasant took off and flew back toward the cover behind them. As Russell watched, two more took wing, then a small cock followed by another pair of hens. Pheasants can be the toughest of birds to flush a second time, but Russell had a good idea where they would be headed this late in the day: He remembered a little tamarack swamp where they liked to roost up. He whistled to his Brit and turned back, already planning his approach. It took him a moment to realize that Pearl was still standing in the field, staring at the spot where the pheasants had taken wing. Russell knew his dog: There was another bird there—maybe a wise old rooster that knew when to fly and when to hide.

In the waist-high pigweed of the cornfield's margin Pearl's point went from tentative to solid. Russell circled wide in front of the dog and waited. In the frozen weeds there was a rustling that had an almost bell-like quality, then the bird stopped. One very long moment stretched into the next. He grinned: This was the part he loved best. He shuffled his feet and brought the rooster clattering into the snowy sky, cackling obscenities and spewing a white stream behind it. This was an exceptionally big, long-tailed cock bird. Sometimes even good shots miss: Russell did, but he held deliberately under the bird with his second barrel, and although his shot drew feathers, the pheasant kept going, following the field edge, coasting beyond the fence, then flapping again to climb over a stand of cedars, then, suddenly—falling. It was easily three hundred yards away.

"Hey, you! Get outta here!"

A man was yelling from the next field. Russell hadn't noticed how close he had come to the buildings of the dairy farm.

"This is posted land. How'd you get in here?"

I'll go talk to him, Russell thought. *The jig is up. Maybe I can apologize my way out of this.* He opened his gun and started toward the angry man, but Pearl was after the crippled pheasant. After a moment's indecision, Russell turned and followed the dog. Behind him, the yelling became indistinct. He didn't look back.

Even though it was still a half-hour before sunset, the snowfall made for a false dusk. If the angry farmer was going to make some calls, maybe a quick exit was in order—after all, the truck was the better part of a mile away. But Pearl was tracking the finest rooster he had shot all season, the kind Mister John would have called a "real dragon." From the look of the bird's tracks, there was nothing wrong with its running ability—the footprints in the snow were twelve inches apart. Russell hurried to stay with Pearl. This last bird at Mister John's was not going to end up as fox bait.

IT HAD GOTTEN colder. The beaver pond was skimmed with ice as Russell crossed the dam in the dark. Trophies are not often a part of bird hunting, but in his left hand Russell carried the last bird from Mister John's covert. It was a fine old cock pheasant, with long spurs and a half-inch of fringe on its tail feathers. *A real dragon.* All but forgotten were his phantoms of conscience.

He noticed the flashing lights before he reached the laurel thicket. He cursed under his breath but then realized it was a fitting ending to an embarrassing obsession. This was among the alternate endings he had considered. He hefted the pheasant and whistled Pearl in to heel.

Stone Fences

A LADY who would later become my wife sat next to me on a stone wall. We were in the woods on the pretext of locating some spring wildflowers, but I had ulterior motives as well. By an old caved-in cellar hole a lilac bush was in full flower. "Look at that." The lady pointed to the lilac. "Someone must have lived out here in the woods at one time."

For someone who didn't know a lady's slipper from a ladyfinger, her recognition that lilacs are not naturally occurring wildflowers was pretty fair. But I was taken aback for a moment by the implication that she thought the woods in which we were sitting had always been there. People have an inertia-like inability to envision a past much unlike the present. I almost asked her who she supposed had made the stone walls we had been stumbling over all morning. But it was spring, and I was a young man whose fancy had turned to things other than lectures on land use in New England circa 1850. My reply went, "How about that! Aren't you warm with that sweater on?"

ONE HUNDRED AND FIFTY years ago we were an agricultural society, and farming was the way of life for the majority of the people in this country. In Massachusetts alone eighty-five percent of the land was under intense cultivation during the time of the Civil War. That figure seems an impossible exaggeration until one walks the hills and woodlands: Nearly every acre of land is laced with stone walls—stone fences, some call them. They climb all but the steepest of hills, edge swamps and bogs, and attest to the fact that farmers' fields existed wherever there was enough topsoil for a root to take hold. They delineated yesterday's hayfields and gardens, rye and cornfields, and orchards and pastures where the rocks were too numerous or too huge to be cleared. Stone fences created cattle runs that channeled cows from barn to distant grazing fields. They bordered lanes and figure prominently on old deeds marking the boundaries of a man's land.

Unlike those of wood and wire, stone fences were permanent, but that fact had little to do with why they were constructed in the first place. Dick Glidden, a displaced New Hampshire-ite, explained it to me this way: "My fatha' needed fences to keep the cows where they b'longed, but it was the depression and we didn't have money for bobbed wi'a. Now, we had those stones to be cleared from the property, and the shortest distance to carry 'em was to the edge of the field. Well, we started linin' up those rocks an' pretty soon we didn't need that bobbed wi'a afta' all. I imagine that's how farm'as had been doin' things for generations."

With that in mind, one can begin to understand why there was no "north forty" on stone country farms. Fields were small. Even an acre can seem huge when a boulder has to be rolled to its edge. The settlers of the Northeast must have quickly discovered that the limiting factor in laying out any field was the number and size of the rocks that had to be cleared from the land.

And New England's stones can be persistent. My own experience with them came during the five years I owned a home on what used to be a farm in Wilbraham. Each spring, after the winter frosts had run their course, there would be a few new rocks showing in the lawn. Some were low enough for the mower to skim over, and I would have won a year's reprieve. But they grew farther out of the ground each winter, and eventually there was nothing else to do but attack them with shovel and pinch bar. By the time I sold that house I had a small stone wall of my own started along the woodline, and the rocks showed no signs of abating their siege on the lawn. I mowed just under an acre. The work that went on on a fifty-acre farm must have been onerous.

SOME STONE FENCES are little more than linear rock piles: After nearly breaking his back carrying a chunk of granite out of the way of his plow, a farmer understandably would probably want nothing more than to just drop it. But here and there some truly artistic stone walls can be found. A century of winter ice and frost will break down any unstable pile, so there was more than a little skill that went into the construction of an enduring wall. Each rock had to be fitted against its neighbor to permit for seasonal expansion and contraction, and slanted toward the center for a self-stabilizing effect.

In the town of Hampden there is a wonderful example of a well-engineered wall. It stands shoulder-high and has nearly perpendicular squared sides, and although the fields it bordered are long since overgrown, it runs through the woodland for a mile or more. The wall is completely intact except for a gap here and there where some huge and long since rotted forest tree fell. Only the scattered stones testify to the breach's violent creation. Mister Hancock, who owns part of the land, tells me that the wall was there seventy years ago when he was a boy, and nobody then remembered who the artisan was. It endures today. Someone, long ago, knew how to build to last.

IMAGINE for a moment living on a farm in the nineteenth century: Farming before the age of electricity was a bitter business. There were no machines to help with the work, no roads to speak of, no telephones and virtually no mail service. Each rural family had to be self-reliant if it was to survive. Some did not. There was no oil truck to call if fuel ran low, and no corner store to run to for a loaf of bread. Insecticides and fertilizers were unknown. Each family did things for themselves, from "putting food by" and laying in a supply of firewood for the winter to setting a broken leg or building a house. The work, all of it, was done by hand. Farm life was more than hard, it was a continuous cycle of drudgery. People literally worked themselves to death. Is it any wonder that two years of servitude and poor rations on a whaling ship seemed attractive to farm boys from New England? Summer, fall, and winter each brought its own particular type of toil, but spring was the time of the hardest work: There was plowing to be done, but first the rocks that the winter had heaved up had to be cleared from the fields.

The west was opening up all through the 1800s. News would eventually reach even the most remote countryman, either through the monthly gazette or simply by word of mouth, and the promise of land free-for-the-settling tempted him, no matter how deeply his roots ran in the poor soil of his hill farm. Perhaps it was the first walk through his fields after the snow cleared that finally convinced the stone country farmer to quit. When a man has cleared rocks from the same fields every spring of his life, he knows that this spring's crop of stones won't be the last: There will be more next spring, and more the spring after that. Tempted by the lure of the West's free land, he might have returned to the farmhouse and said, "Hell an' tarnation, Sarah." (Or whatever it was that farmers used to say to their wives back then.) "Let's chuck this place and go to Oregon." Or Nebraska. Or California. Or any of the other places that his farmers' dreams were made of.

If there were no buyers for the place, and frequently there were none for the worn-out hill farms, it was simply abandoned. The family cemetery was left behind. It sometimes contained ten or more generations. The barn that Grandpa built, the new apple trees that should start producing next season, Mother's lilac bush and the years of toil and worry were left where they lay. The Conestoga wagons that rolled westward were manned by hale farming families from the Northeast. Although they carried much with them, they left far more behind. Ahead were Indians and tornados and droughts and sod deeper than a plow could bite, but they pushed on. To a New England stone farmer, the promise of rich flat land with no rocks to clear was lure enough. Like the boys who ran away to sign on whaling ships, the unknown had more to offer than the life they left behind.

NOT ALL the farms were abandoned. Modern dairy farms and orchards still dot the countryside from Maine to Pennsylvania, but they are located in the few prime farming areas, usually the deep topsoil of river valleys or flatlands. Even a hundred years ago these were "good" farms, where a man could grow something other than rocks.

But in the hills, Nature quickly reclaimed the abandoned land. The fields grew to gray birch and popple within a few seasons. Sumac and juniper followed the weeds into the dooryard. The old lanes grew over and were forgotten as the natural course of forest succession saw hardwoods sprout in the shade of the lesser trees. Woodland animals, which had been gradually displaced since the first fields were cleared centuries before, now returned; ruffed grouse flourished in the second growth, the beaver ended his northern exile, and whitetail deer, nearly extinct in New England in 1860, prospered.

Remnants persist; apple trees, unlike the farmer's other crops, needed little attention and thrive to this day throughout the Northeast. The woodlands are sprinkled with monstrous oaks that could only have developed their spreading character by growing in the open for a century or more. But there is not much to be found of the old farms themselves. Reforestation has completely changed the landscape, and rust and rot and the passing seasons have a way of pulling down the accomplishments of men. Sometimes a stone or two remains erect in the woodland, marking what was once a family graveyard. Of the houses and outbuildings, only the foundations remain under the moss and ground pine. And a few woody old lilacs and rosebushes continue to bloom each spring near what used to be the kitchen windows of those farmhouses, having outlived the dreams of the farm wives who planted them. They bear silent testimony to the fact that someone did indeed ". . . live out here at one time."

But of all the vestiges of these ancient farms, the most ubiquitous and enduring are the stone fences. They are the result of a way of life that no longer exists. But, like the wear marks and sweat stains on some well-used tool, theirs is a story obvious to anyone who will take the time to read it.

Wellfleet

It's a wicked wind
And it chills me to the bone,
And if you do not believe me
Come and gaze upon the shadow at your door.

—Gordon Lightfoot

HER MOANS awoke him. In the darkness he reached out and shook her shoulder. "Wake up, Cynthia—it's just a bad dream."

She spun around to face him, caught somewhere between nightmare and reality. For a dark moment she didn't recognize him.

"Hey, you were dreaming. It's me—remember?"

She sighed in recognition and laid her head against his chest.

"It's okay, Kiddo," he whispered. "Whatever it was is over and gone. I'm here—it's only me."

She clung to him tightly. When the fright had evaporated and her breathing had returned to normal, she said, "It's not true."

"What's not?"

"The 'only' part."

In the darkness he held her closer.

THE DOG followed Robert across the asphalt apron to the edge of the grassy lot, her tail wagging. He whistled to her and motioned "go ahead," then stood waiting with his hands thrust into his pockets against the morning chill. Unhurriedly, the setter sniffed the scent of the previous evening's rabbits and field mice. "Come on, Suzie—make it quick," he muttered.

Suddenly the dog's expression intensified, and she moved a few stiff-legged steps into a firm point in front of an old apple tree. Reluctant to believe what he was seeing, Robert glanced back toward the inn, unsure whether he hoped someone was watching or glad no one was. He walked through the knee-high grass to where his dog stood and flushed the little covey of quail she had found. A half-dozen birds darted into the air in random directions, but then formed into a loose flock as they flew together toward the woods beyond the road.

He stood watching the birds fly off, smiling to himself.

THE DOOR to the room opened before he could get his key into the lock. Cynthia was still barefoot, but had dressed in poplin chinos and a chamois shirt and had pinned her hair up under the cap he had brought for her. She kissed him, then stood for a moment in his embrace.

"Hi, Kiddo," he said. When she didn't answer, his tone changed. "What's the matter, Cynthia?"

"Do you feel this lost when you come to the city?" She spoke without lifting her head from his shoulder.

"Having the toilet down the hall doesn't suit you, I guess."

"Oh, no." She hurried to deny it. "It's not that: It's lovely here— 'quaint,' I guess is the right word. I just feel I'm a guest in your private world—I know you're as much a visitor here as I am, but you seem a part of all this."

He thought for a moment before answering. "Yes, I guess that's the way I feel when we're in the city together: You belong there, and I'm out of my element." After a moment, he went to his open suitcase and began gathering the few items they would need for the day's outing. "I almost didn't recognize you when I walked in. You look like a model in an Orvis catalog."

"This is my 'fashionable huntress' outfit." She knelt to pet the dog. "Hi, Suzie . . . Oh, you're all wet."

"It's frosty out there," he answered for his setter. After a moment he asked, "What are you going to wear for boots, Cynthia?"

"I was waiting to see what you'd suggest—I borrowed those . . ." She indicated a pair of cold weather pacs with felt liners. ". . . and I've got my old Frys."

"We're going to be doing quite a bit of walking, so I know you can't wear these." He held up the pacs. "Whatever the others are, they're it."

Leaning against the bureau, she began to pull on a pair of leather boots that had been designed to weather urban winters in high style. "They're *real* comfortable," she replied to his skeptical look.

"Oh, I'm sure they are. But when I said you should bring boots, I was thinking more in terms of L. L. Bean rather than Lord & Taylor."

"Bonwit-Teller," she corrected.

He zipped closed the small canvas duffle he had filled and slung a canvas jacket over his arm. In the corner of the room the setter watched Robert. Sensing it was time to go, she went to the door to be let out.

In the parking lot he opened the liftback of her sports car and put his cased shotgun and the duffle inside, then let his setter in to sit on the floor of the passenger side. Hers was the only car with out-of-state plates, and shared the lot with just his mud-spattered pick-up and a couple of nondescript station wagons, one with the name of the inn lettered on the door. The Supra, sleek and gleaming, seemed so unrelated to the other vehicles that it might have been a rocket ship from outer space.

Driving out, he slowed and pointed out the stunted apple tree. "Suzie found a little covey of quail by that tree this morning when I took her out."

"Yes. I saw you from the window."

He glanced across at her before muttering a disconnected "Oh." She hadn't made mention of the fact. Her reluctance, at times, to initiate even the most idle conversations held a puzzling fascination for him. *Fascination*, he thought to himself: a good word. Certainly more accurate than, say, *love*. He had always lived with quiet personalities all around him, but Cynthia's shyness went beyond the dictionary definition of quiet. She could be clever and quick, but it was her silences that intrigued him—not that he wanted to emulate her, but rather it was the effortlessness with which she hid her thoughts—something he could never do.

As ROBERT opened the door of the coffee shop, the dozen or so obviously local people seated around the counter turned and stared openly at them. The men still wore their hats. Robert waved. "Hi. How's everybody this morning?" There were nods and scattered mumbles that passed for return greetings as the crowd turned back to their conversations and newspapers. Robert and Cynthia sat at the far end of the counter.

"How come you do that?" She spoke quietly.

"What? Talk to strangers?"

She nodded.

"It was either that or give 'em the finger. When people stare at me, I just can't ignore them." He shrugged as he spoke.

A buxom waitress set a pair of empty mugs on the counter in front of them. "Two coffees?"

"She'll have a hot chocolate, please." He had previously gotten used to answering for both of them when in public. The waitress filled his cup from a pot beneath the counter, then retrieved Cynthia's and padded off heavily toward a suspicious plastic machine that dispensed what passed for hot cocoa.

Cynthia sat with her elbows together, her hands folded against her mouth. "Ooo, bismarcks!" She indicated the display case across from them.

"Looks like some heavy-duty calories to me," he muttered back.

"That doesn't bother me: I have this low-sodium diet." Knowing he was looking at her, she made a little flirting move, licking her lips with the tip of her tongue. Robert smiled and squeezed her knee beneath the counter.

The waitress returned and set the mug in front of Cynthia, then looked at Robert: "And . . .?"

"One of those cream-filled things there, and an apple jelly doughnut."

After they were served she leaned toward him. "Apple? Are you turning into some kind of health nut or something?"

He grinned, then said in mock disgust, "The things I do for you: doughnuts for breakfast!" He shook his head. "I want you to know that the aromas coming out of that kitchen this morning nearly did a number on my resolve."

"Oh, I meant to tell you—that Mrs. Eldridge phoned while you were out with Suzie to see if we were coming down to breakfast."

"What'd you tell her?"

"I said no." She paused, remembering. "You know, she said something like 'the bacon is cut extra lean today'—even after what you said to her yesterday."

"Oh, don't worry about her. There's a lot of people, especially motherly types like her, that think there's something wrong with you if you don't eat meat. They figure if they can just make it enticing enough they'll cure you of your bad habit." He smiled, then added, "But you know all about that. She probably takes it personally if her guests don't show up for her meals."

She turned toward him. "Just the same, there's no reason for you to stop eating things you like just because . . ."

He stopped her. "We've been through that before." Out of respect for her preferences, he adjusted his own diet whenever he was with her. He left a silence, then said, "How about a bite of your bismarck?"

THEY DROVE northward on the back roads, with Robert behind the wheel of her Supra. The morning was gloriously clear, almost like something contrived by a travel agent to demonstrate how lovely this particular part of New England could be in autumn. Robert downshifted, then accelerated out of a tight turn. The road left the scrub pine woods and ran along a stretch of open marshland. He pulled the gearshift back into fourth, then laughed out loud in exhilaration. "You drive like you feel—did you ever notice that?" He looked across at her. "There are those days when you're down and you putter along at twenty-five, but with you here this is definitely a sixty-on-the-straightaway sort of day."

Cynthia's reply was a smile. He waited for her to pick up the conversation, but the silence lengthened. Her shy manner could be disconcerting at times when he felt like talking, but he had learned to resist the temptation to read meanings into her silences: Being uncommonly quiet, she just wasn't given to idle chatter. Three years earlier it had been that trait that had caused him to dislike her upon first meeting: Unexpressive and reserved almost to the point of indifference, she reminded him of a beautiful but untalented actress. And it had seemed that she simply wasn't interested in him. He was, after all, a decade older than she and married, neither fact of which he tried to hide. Only when events brought them together again did he begin to see through the quiet exterior. His initial assessment had been wrong. Cynthia seemed a contradiction: shyness with a less evident self-assurance. Her intellect became evident the longer he knew her, yet she retained as her most singular trait something that could only be termed girlishness. She was sure enough of her femininity that she sometimes wore men's cologne. And, unlike every other woman Robert had known, she actually looked *better* with her clothes off. He smiled inwardly, remembering. There are times when strangers hurry toward one another before issues of personality can cloud intimacy and desire, but it seemed he only grew more charmed the more he learned of her. It's a rare man who can turn his back on the best thing he's ever had. Robert couldn't.

"What are you smiling about, Robert?"

He took his eyes from the road for a moment. "I was doing that just to get your attention. If that didn't work, the Donald Duck imitations were next."

Cynthia laughed. "I talk when I've got something to say, unlike somebody else in this car—and I don't mean *you*, Suzie." She reached down and petted the dog sitting at her feet.

"I was thinking about a lady I met at a seminar in New York City—back three years ago or so."

For a long moment she seemed to be listening to her own thoughts. "I had a hard time accepting you at face value at first. That was a bad period in my life—I had just about given up on myself when you came along. You were something I had never seen before: Someone I cared about who actually cared about me in return. The situation you were in didn't exactly make things easy for me, you know."

He nodded, smiling a tight-lipped smile.

"There have been other people in and out of my life since then.

Some things don't change, though. You're still the only man I've ever really loved." She touched his arm as she finished.

There were three years of anguish and indecisiveness bound up in any reply he might make. He nodded again but said nothing.

HE TURNED OFF the pavement and followed a gravel road for a half-mile. When they passed an open field, he slowed and pulled to the side. "This looks like the place," he said after a moment's study, and shut the engine off.

"You've been here before?"

"Oh, no. It just *looks* birdy. There ought to be some quail in here."

The dog, sitting on the floor at Cynthia's feet, had been sedate until Robert shut off the engine. She immediately sat up, trembling in anticipation of the hunt.

The odor of a nearby salt marsh hung on the light breeze. He strapped a bell on the dog's collar, then uncased his shotgun and closed the liftback. "This is the gun I was telling you about—here, have a look. . . ." He held the opened double out to her.

"It's lovely—the wood is almost like a jewel." She declined to take the shotgun, as he knew she would: She was afraid without being fascinated.

"The gun's a luxury—no two ways about it—but it's the sort of thing that's real easy to get used to."

"That's just the way I feel about my car." She glanced back at the Supra. Even parked on the shoulder, it appeared to be fluid motion stopped for an instant in time. "I spent a long time waiting for a car like that; all those years in school without one, then I had that old Volkswagen when I was first in New York." She glanced at him, flirting now. "You remember that car, don't you?"

"You never heard me complain about that old bug—it got us around, and was pretty good at keeping secrets."

She smiled the dimpled smile he had come to believe she reserved only for him.

They walked the edge of the field, following the natural boundary formed by the woodline that curved back toward a little freshwater pond. The dog worked the open cover at a tireless run, her tail a waving flag in the tall grass. There were wild cranberries growing like ground cover along the back of the field, and sumac trees with much of their autumn color already on the ground. The few leaves that remained on the branches glowed almost luminescently crimson in the morning sunlight. They found a small flock of waxwings in some cedar scrub but no quail. They were back at the car in an hour.

Cynthia leaned against the car, pulling off the burrs that had stuck to the cuffs of her pants. "So *this* is hunting." She teased him with mock sarcasm.

"You know it, Kiddo. It's the most enjoyable thing I can do with my clothes on." He grinned at her. "So far all we've done is take a walk, but we'll find some birds before the morning's out." He looked out over the field they had just been through. "Still, I can't believe there aren't any quail here: It looks like such good cover."

"What would you have done if we had found some?"

"What do you mean, 'What would I have done?' What do you think the gun's for? I'd have shot one or two—or at least tried to."

"Wouldn't you be giving the birds more of a sporting chance if you let them fly first?"

For a moment he looked into her face, expecting a sign that she was joking. She wasn't. He left a silence, trying to decide how properly to reply. "Cynthia, I *do* flush the birds before I shoot at them. Sportsmanship is what bird hunting is all about—without it none of this would have much meaning." He became aware of his own body language and sat beside her on the trunk transom.

She was embarrassed and said nothing.

"Look, I'm just beginning to realize that you know next to nothing about all this, but maybe during the next few days I can show you why this hunting business means as much in my life as it does." Taking her hand, he said, "It's important to me that you understand. Be patient, Kiddo."

She paused before saying, "You too."

"THERE'S SOME DUCKS over there." She pointed out the car window toward a small cove. He slowed to a stop on a wooden bridge across an estuary and studied the distant birds.

"Those are brant."

"I thought I was doing pretty well just knowing they're not sea gulls."

He smiled. "They're little geese that only live on the coast."

"Do you hunt them?"

"I used to, but they've closed the season on brant for the last couple of years. Their population is down. Evidently a blight killed off most of the eelgrass, and they won't eat anything else."

"They'd rather die than go off their diet? Sounds like my kind of goose."

ROBERT slowed his pace when he noticed Cynthia was hurrying to keep up with him. His setter had found a covey along the edge of some scrub oaks five minutes before. He had circled Suzie's point, sacrificing a chance for a shot to keep the birds from retreating into the woods. The field where the covey had pitched in was a tangle of low bayberry bushes and plum thickets—difficult walking, but at least there would be a chance for a clear shot when the scattered birds were found. Suzie covered the ground in front of them with her head high, looking back only at the completion of each cast. Even when the brush screened the dog, they followed the setter's course by listening to the bell on her collar.

"Does Suzie see the birds when she points them?"

"No. It's a matter of her scenting them with her nose. It's not smelling, but some other sense that humans don't have." Like all his other attempts to explain bird hunting, his explanation had not expressed his idea well, and he was bothered. He rephrased the thought. "Hunting dogs are bred for their ability to use their noses, and while there are a lot of other things expected of a bird dog, without that superrefined ability the other things don't matter—they have to find birds." He spoke without taking his eyes from the setter's progress. "Understand that Suzie is the best dog I've ever had . . . Ever *will have*, probably."

"You said you only owned female dogs."

He nodded. "The only dog I had that didn't turn out well was a male. Bitches tend to be less hardheaded and easier to train."

"Why do you call them that?"

Robert looked at her out of the corner of his eye. "Bitches?"

She nodded.

"It's a proper term." He paused, then added, "I wonder why women are so sensitive about that word?"

"Probably for the same reason you're sensitive about the word ass-hole."

He paused a moment, then laughed out loud. With his arm around her shoulders he hugged her to him. "Smart ass," he said, and they giggled together. "You know, I think I like the silent Cynthia much better." Her ability to make him laugh always crept up on him—he was never quite prepared for it.

Minutes later the dog found the first of the singles from the scattered covey. From full stride she skidded into a point that resembled a lawn chair clumsily unfolded, and the abruptness of the stop made Cynthia gasp audibly. Suzie stood transfixed, head low, tail straight up. Somewhere in the thicket in front of her a quail crouched, equally transfixed.

"Are you watching?"

She nodded, and Robert stepped toward the dog's point.

SUZIE LAY on the floor of the car, snoozing with her head resting on the transmission. The past hour had been sprinkled with birds and points and feathers floating among the scrub pine. As Robert drove, he whistled the melody of a Jim Croce song he had heard earlier in the day. He became aware that Cynthia was listening intently and tapered off.

"It's still true, you know," she said.

"What is?"

"That song: 'Once We Were Lovers.' We still are as far as I'm concerned, even if I *don't* see you as often as I'd like." She put her hand over his on the gearshift.

He listened to his own thoughts for a moment. "'Once.' Not so very long ago, but once—as in 'once upon a time.'"

As was her wont, when she had nothing to say she said nothing.

After a minute he addressed the silence. "Why haven't you ever asked me for anything?"

"Like what?"

"Like leave my wife and live with you."

A silence hung in the air for a long moment before she answered. "I guess I'm not so sure I'd want that, or that's what you'd want, either. I like things the way they are: We're friends, just like we've always been."

"Once we were lovers." His voice was flat.

She made no reply. The silence lengthened.

"I'm sorry," he said. "I shouldn't play semantical games. I just think I deserve a better answer than that."

She was slow to reply, and didn't answer his question directly. "You wouldn't leave your wife."

"I'm glad one of us is sure of that."

Again she made no reply.

His grip on the wheel tightened. "What is it that you're so afraid of? Or is it a matter of 'He can't have said no if I've never asked'?"

There was an abrupt change in her tone. "What is it? Do you *want* me to ask you to leave your wife?"

"No. Only why you haven't."

"Do you think I like being the 'other woman'? I know your wife—I dream of her, and in my dream *I'm* the evil one. Everything I know about her has come through you, and the image you've put in my mind is of a loving woman. You've never said, 'My wife doesn't care any more' or 'There's no love in our marriage.' No. You love her, and it shows. I don't doubt that you love me too, but it's her you belong to. I'm no fool, Robert: There's no future for us, and there is no good answer to your question, only might-have-beens and apologies."

They drove on, separated by the charged cloud of their silence. After a long minute he said, "Still in all, you never even asked me. Were you that sure of my answer?" He looked across at her, but her gaze was fixed somewhere beyond him. She turned and looked out the side window, taking her hand from his as she did.

IN A VILLAGE he parked the car along the main street. From across the square the town clock chimed five times. With a questioning look Cynthia reached across and pushed his sleeve up to read his watch.

"Ships' time," he answered. "How about if we have lunch here?" He indicated a restaurant across the street.

She nodded, then removed her cap, shaking her head as she did so that her hair fell loosely into place.

On the rooftops and in the nearly bare branches of the few trees on the common, a flock of crows patrolled, calling to each other or perhaps just at the world in general. As Robert and Cynthia crossed the street something out on the marsh caught the crows' attention, and they took wing as if answering to a roll, swooping from their stations one after another until finally only their distant calls remained.

Inside the hostess seated them in an unexpectedly airy dining area that had been glassed in to enclose a small arboretum. Sunlight dappled the tile floor and the dooryard outside. After the waitress had taken their bar order, Cynthia sat staring at the potted flowers beyond the table.

"Hmm," he said. "This is very nice: not a damn antique in sight . . . Very 'off-Cape.'" There was a forced lightness to his manner that only outlined the awkwardness of the moment. She looked directly at him and started to say something, then changed her mind. Instead she reached across the table and touched his face.

He looked down. "I didn't intend to start an argument back there. Really."

"I never would have known." The sarcasm in her voice was gentle. She smiled and took his hand.

"I'm sorry." He felt silly. Then, to change the subject, he asked, "How are your feet holding up in those boots?"

"Okay."

"After the walking we've done, you can see that you never would have made it in those heavy pacs. They're more for things like ice fishing or . . ."

She touched his lips to stop him. After a moment she said, "Sometimes we make our greatest demands of others by asking of them nothing at all."

He looked at her across the table, not sure of her meaning. Unblinking, she returned his gaze. "What's that?" he asked.

"The answer you asked me for."

Robert mulled over her sentiments in an unsettled silence as they waited for the waitress to bring their drinks. He had no reply.

AS THEY APPROACHED the inn, one of the old station wagons was in the driveway, waiting to turn out to the left. In the wagon Mrs. Eldridge rolled down the car window, and he stopped alongside her car as he pulled in.

"Did you find many birds?" She looked past Cynthia to speak to him through the open windows. She pronounced "birds" with a broad "a."

"Two coveys," Robert answered.

"I hope you brought some back with you."

He nodded. "Five."

"Well, that'll be enough for the two of you. Just leave them on the porch there, and I'll take care of them. I've a lovely quail recipe with cranberry stuffing: If you don't mind eating just a bit late, I'll fix them for your dinner . . ." She paused a moment, considering. "That is, if it's all right with you." She looked at Cynthia.

"Yes, I'd like that very much," Cynthia replied.

Mrs. Eldridge tooted a short good-bye on the horn as the station wagon drove off. He parked the car, then looked at Cynthia for a long moment before speaking. "Why did you tell her that?"

Cynthia busied herself gathering their gear from the car. "Oh, you know I eat fish, and sometimes chicken. It's no big deal."

"You know it is." When she made no reply, he said, "I realize how squeamish you can be about these things: You don't have to do this for me. Sure, I've asked you to try to understand why hunting means so much in my life, and it's been evident all afternoon that you're trying to see it through my eyes. But if you're really going to have those quail for supper, I want it to be for the right reasons—because *you* want to, not because you think I've asked you to. Don't you see?"

He searched inside her eyes for a glimpse of understanding, but the answer he found there was not addressed to his question. She said quietly, "Don't you?"

The Tarnished RXP

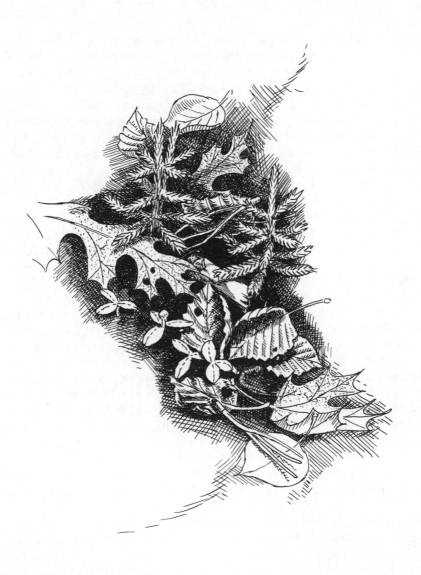

You and I can share
The silence,
Finding comfort together,
The way old friends do.

—Benny Anderson and Bjorn Ulvaeus

A GLINT of blue showed through the fallen leaves of the dry bog a few paces in front of him. Without taking his eyes off his young springer, he bent and picked up the bit of trash. It was an old empty, a Peters RXP case. The brass head was badly tarnished, but, as is both the blessing and the curse of all plastic, the hull was none the worse for its seasons on the forest floor. "Hmm?" He raised a questioning eyebrow. "Someone else hunts here?" The only other person he had ever seen in the Brook Covert was an old trapper who worked the streams, but here was evidence that memories made here were part of someone else's repertoire. The still-reloadable shell went into his gamebag, where it clinked dully with the empties from the morning's hunt.

He thought of the Brook Covert as his own. It was far enough from the road to be as private as any piece of open land can be. He and Dick had discovered it years ago and had hunted grouse and woodcock here together for as long as Dick had lived. The place centered around the confluence of a pair of bog-fed brooks. The old gent who owned the land had told them of a stand of virgin paper birch that had stood on the rise between the brooklets. Back during the Depression the stand had provided saw logs when no other money was to be had. Afterward the farmer had put in an orchard among the stumps. Most of the old apple trees still remained, over-grown now with sumac and white pine. But the heart of the covert was in the broad flat valley below the orchard, where the brooklets joined and woodcock favored the moist ground beneath the aspens. Now, with Dick gone, he continued to hunt their "private" covert alone. Another man's name was on the legal deed in the town offices, but years of memories gave him squatter's rights on the place.

Ahead of him the springer's tail wagged furiously as she sniffed at a chipmunk in a rock wall. He grinned at the pup's exuberance but added a touch of authority to his "Move on!"

Years before Rusty had found a cripple they'd given up for lost in that same stone wall—he'd done his share of mousing around as a

pup, too. There could never be another dog like Rusty. Any other
setter he might own would be under the unfair handicap of being
constantly compared to Rusty, so when the time had come to start
another puppy, he had by-passed his prejudices by choosing a flushing dog. The springer took some getting used to, but he was having
more fun training the pup than he would have thought possible.

As he picked his way over the rocks of the wall, he thought back
on some of the remarkable memories this place held for him. He had
stood in awe, unable to act, as a goshawk pursued a grouse on the
wing—it had been Dick's warning shot that had scared off the predator. Another time, up in the old orchard, neither he nor his partner
had noticed the porcupine on the ground until Rusty had jumped
over it on his way to make a retrieve. The old setter had a lifelong love/
hate relationship with porkies, and he had held his breath until Dick's
hand had closed around the setter's collar.

Ah, memories. He smiled to himself. Although he had often
times hunted alone in years past, it seemed that the easy-going personality of his hunting partner was an integral part of nearly all of his
recollections—memorable things just seemed to happen when Dick
had been along. Or perhaps it was simply a matter of his being able to
appreciate things more fully when they had been shared with the sort
of man Dick had been. He had hunted with others after Dick's death,
but a friendship a lifetime in the making is not easily replaced, and he
found he was more comfortable hunting alone.

The valley began to broaden out before him. He found an inviting
fallen tree trunk and sat for a moment to rest and remember. He
opened his shotgun and laid it aside in exchange for his pipe and
tobacco. The springer, grown accustomed to her master's frequent rest
stops, came in and sat at his feet.

There would be no woodcock in the valley today. At this late date
they would long since have departed for points south. But he recalled
another day in this same valley when he and Dick had paused right
along in here to change loads in expectation of flight birds. Old Rusty
had been late in his prime that year, so it must have been either '74 or
'75. He shook his head. God! In 1975 Rusty might well have been the
finest grouse dog in the state. That day the setter's walking point had
signaled "grouse" rather than the expected woodcock, but they stayed
with their 9s as they followed behind the point—they had been caught
with open guns at inopportune moments before. The pair of grouse
Rusty corralled quickly lost their nerve in the open understory: Theirs
was not the paired flush of grouse on calendar pictures and magazine
covers but the more typical "you-go-that-way-and-I'll-go-this" of

smart hunter-wary birds. One of the grouse came his way, and as his shot folded the bird, he heard the report of Dick's 12 to his left. Rusty went to fetch Dick's bird, so he had walked the scant dozen paces to make his own retrieve. He and Rusty arrived at Dick's side together, each with a grouse, but Dick hadn't realized they had shared a double or even that two birds had flushed—he was futilely searching for his empty shell in the leaves. The confused expression on his partner's face was as clear in his memory as if it had happened yesterday rather than five years ago.

He got to his feet, stretched, and picked up his gun. The young springer recognized the signs and bounded off, eager to be on with the hunt. The memory of the shared double lingered as he replaced the pair of shells in the barrels. It had all happened just a few yards behind him, and he turned and glanced back the way he had come. In his gamebag the empty shells clinked.

It was then that his mind made the connection. "I wonder . . ." he muttered aloud. He reached back into his gamebag and brought out the old blue empty. It held his gaze for a long moment. On the spent primer was what was left of the adhesive paper dot that Dick had used to mark his reloads.

He smiled, slowly this time, and sat back on the log. The springer came in and nudged his hand impatiently. He reached out and scratched the dog's ears, but he was alone with his thoughts.

The past lives, he thought. It is a reality. Sometimes embellished, often regretted, more frequently simply forgotten. But it was there, and it was real. In his hand he held a touchstone that affirmed that fact. Life is for the living, it's true, but the past is another reality where a man can hunt again with dogs now sleeping and men who live only in the minds of those who remember them.

On the entire face of the earth there was only one person to whom the tarnished RXP meant anything. He wrapped it in his handkerchief and buttoned the flap of his shirt pocket over it. Like all souvenirs, it was singularly unextraordinary. But it said to him alone, *"We were together when it happened—Remember?"*

He patted the shell in his pocket. He remembered.

Branta Canadensis
Northeaster

DAD RUNS DOWN the check list while I act out his Doubting Thomas role, digging through the assembled gear to find an item for him that I know is there.

"Spare tire for the trailer?"

"Here, in the boat."

"Anchor and rope?"

"Right here."

"Oars?"

"Check."

"Gas can?"

"Here."

"Is it full, Steve?"

"All set." I glance at the gauge and twist the cap to be sure it's loosened for the trip. The check-off job is usually fairly simple when I'm going waterfowling alone, but it runs to a bit more detail when two men are going overnight. The job is further complicated by the constant stream of suggestions from the porch, where my mother stands with my wife, both slightly more than spectators.

"Did you remember some food for the dog?"

I wave a can of Ken-L-Ration at my wife.

"If you were smart, you'd open it up now and just put a plastic cover over it."

I don't mind her suggestion so much as her being right. I go into the house and run the can through the opener.

We finish the inventory, and I let Win out of the back yard. Her kennelmate barks a protest at being left behind. Both dogs have been pacing the gate in eager anticipation since Dad arrived. Win runs to the truck and sits on the floor, afraid to misbehave at this crucial time. She trembles with excitement.

My mother is there to drive Dad's car back home. She has a last-minute suggestion. "Hank, where's the stuff for your contacts?"

"In with the gun cleaning gear, I think."

Ultimately we'll need to be sure, so I dig into our equipment again. Dad will need his eye drops out on the marsh, so they shouldn't be in the reserve bag anyway. I look through its contents to be sure there are no other surprises. "You'll be needing these too, Dad." I turn up a box of goose loads.

"Naw. If I need some, I'll borrow a few of yours."

I transfer the box into the knapsack we'll carry with us. My own three-inch loads will not fit in Dad's gun. He knows this.

Goose shooting and Dad don't get along any more. Because we live far inland, our waterfowling trips to the coast are reduced to once- or twice-a-season excursions, and nearly all our goose hunting is tied into these trips. Dad has seen all of his sons take geese and has had his own share of opportunities. Not overly many, to be sure, but enough to feel haunted by his constant misses. And missing becomes doubly painful when those around you are not: Five years earlier my brother and I crouched in a tidal cut waiting out a flock of Canadas, and when we stood to take our first geese, only he was successful. We had both waited years for that moment, but he contained his own exuberance when he saw the look of abject disappointment on my face. Two seasons and several geese later mine was the only goose to fall from a flaring flock. When I turned and clapped my father on the back, mirrored in his face was the same emotion I had felt at my own first easy miss. So I wisely said no more. Since then geese have become not so much an obsession as a dream with Dad—things he is not entirely certain are real. He is far from a poor shot, yet each missed opportunity seemed to inhibit the next until no shot was too easy to be missed. He was more embarrassed by his failings than he would admit.

I DRIVE the truck on the interstate. Since his eye operation Dad isn't much of a night driver. We talk, mostly of the next day, but after a while I hear his head nodding against the door window. There was a time when he took his sons hunting. Now they take him.

The drive takes three hours, but most of it is on main highways. Dad wakes with a start as the tires roar on the steel gratings of the drawbridge. I snap on the high beams as we turn onto the marsh road. A red fox is caught for a moment in the lights before he slips into the bayberry tangles along the roadside. One more duck hunter on the marsh.

With the truck parked, the three of us get out to stretch our legs. After hours with the noise of the truck in my ears the silence is deafening. Gradually I begin to hear the sigh of the wind through the beach grass, the sound of distant high-tide breakers rolling in beyond the dunes, the squall of a heron that Win scares up along the water. The clouds of tomorrow's predicted northeaster have gathered, and the first raindrop hits my nose.

"Look at this." I point toward the light spot in the cloud cover where the moon has been blocked out. A small flock of geese is laboring by, on their way out to the marsh. In the whisper of the wind we can hear their occasional squawk, then the creaking of their wings as they pass close to us. The darkness quickly swallows them, but Dad continues to stare out onto the salt flats until, finally, the wind no longer carries their sounds to us. Which of his misses is he reliving?

"Someday, before it's all over, I'm gonna get one of those sons-a-bitches." He grins at me, but the dream remains in his expression.

THE ALARM wakes me. The wind, off the ocean now, whips rain against the side of the truck. I pull on my woolen bibfronts, then sit in a stupor for a long minute, trying to get my mind working on the problem of what to do next. Outside Dad is working by flashlight. He has on a raincoat, which makes sense to me. I pull my own parka from under my sleeping bag, slip on my old loafers, and step out of the camper-back into the gale. Win comes to greet me, then retreats into the lee of the truck where Dad already has his Coleman stove going. I can smell coffee perking.

"Gonna be a terrific day!" He has the flashlight tucked under his chin and is using both hands to tighten the motor to the transom of the boat. The rain is being driven down at a forty-five-degree angle. How can he be so happy when I'm not even sure if I'm awake?

I pour out two cups of coffee, then go to the truck cab to get out the doughnuts. The floor is littered with bits of paper. I search far under the seat and find the second bag that Win couldn't reach.

"I've got good news and bad news, Dad: Win ate half of our store of doughnuts. The *good* news is that *my* half is okay."

Dad surveys the damage. "Bag and all, huh? She's already had her breakfast, but you'd better get her some water or she'll be drinking from the salt marsh."

I scratch Win behind the ears as she drinks. I'm to blame, really. She had been so gassy on the trip down that I had put her in the cab for the night without remembering that I had stashed our breakfast under the seat. You can't blame a dog for that. Hell, my brother once left a full-grown Lab in his car for twenty minutes and came back to find that his dog had eaten the steering wheel. All that was left was the hub. I pour out a refill for Win. Doughnuts make anybody thirsty. Or maybe it was the wax-paper bag.

FULLY LOADED, the boat sinks down to its last six inches of freeboard. I've often wondered if the Coast Guard would declare us unseaworthy. A small mountain of sacked decoys and equipment all but blocks my forward view from the rear seat. Dad sits facing me amidst the cased guns, gas can, and oars. Win is there too, and I hardly have room for my knees in the cramped compartment.

As we pull away from the launch area, Dad points rearward. Two vehicles pass under the street lamps back on the drawbridge. Each has a boat in tow. Waterfowl aren't the only ones driven onto the marsh by a storm.

We snake our way along the tidal river. Win sits like a compressed spring, watching the ducks that flush at every other turn. They are seen for a moment, then disappear as eyes strain to discern one shade of dark from another in the raining predawn blackness.

The tide continues to run out. We are early but need to be to have water enough to float the boat. With the moon full the tides will be extreme, and the marsh creeks will drain completely before mean low tide at dawn. We battle the current, finding the deepest channels wherever the tide runs swiftest. In two places I get out and walk the boat over sand bars, sounding the water in front of me with an oar as I go.

There are no landmarks on the salt marsh. The daily tides see to that. I navigate by counting turns and forks in the stream. The sameness of the riverbanks is always confusing, more so in the darkness, and even when we have arrived at "the spot," there is nothing to appear familiar.

"Is this it?" I speak above the motor's drone.

"Seems to be." He's not sure either.

We struggle in the boot-sucking mud of the creek bed as we pitch our gear up onto the solid ground above, then climb up after it. Using the anchor rope, I pull the boat into a creek cut where it will be hidden and out of the current of the returning tide.

Our hunting spot is three hundred yards inland, where a series of connected potholes forms a natural retreat for waterfowl in the salt marsh. We divide up the equipment, shoulder our load, and start out, ducking our hat visors into the driving rain as we go.

The wind carries the sounds of geese to us, and as we approach the salt ponds, the Canadas take flight. Win races ahead at the sight of them but suddenly vanishes. She pops back into sight quickly—like us, she is not immune to falling into an unseen hole.

We select a sheltered cove and gather our equipment on an adjoining finger of marsh. The job of setting out the rig goes with practiced ease, despite the darkness and rain. Moving carefully in the crotch-deep water, I position the decoys with a boat oar that doubles as a wading staff. On shore Dad readies the blocks and places each decoy anchor, in turn, into the notched oar I stretch to him. There is no tidal rise and fall in the potholes, and the decoy lines can be matched to the depth of the water. On their five-foot cords I arrange the fifteen decoys into a dense crescent pattern that resembles a tight knot of black ducks at rest, out of the wind. The last three decoys are diminutive teal, two hens and a boldly painted drake green wing. I set them behind the near horn of the crescent. They will be pleasant to watch there, if nothing else.

I walk our four cork goose decoys into the open cove ahead of the crescent, feeling like Gulliver towing the Lilliputians' ships. I arrange them in conjunction with the five stand-up shells that Dad rigs on the shore. By the time I've finished making the few minor adjustments in the rig, Dad has already set up the folding stools back in the grass. I come up behind the spot, careful to walk in Dad's path. There are goose droppings all around us.

We sit down to wait out the hour before shooting time. Gradually darkness gives way to grayness. Several freshwater coots swim into the rig, and Win watches them as intensely as if she were on point. Ducks have been moving since first light. They emerge from the gray, give our rig a quick look, and are quickly gone again. Some like what they see, and at one point we have two pairs of blacks in the rig with the coots. When the passing birds become more than just dark silhouettes, I dig out my pocket watch and am surprised to find that we are but ten minutes from legal shooting time.

Now the water is noticeably brighter, reflecting the lightening sky. The wind, which had abated, picks up once again, mercifully without the accompanying rain. I hear Dad's safety click off and then back on again as a pair of blacks give our rig a once-over. Win has also heard it, and she crouches, waiting for the shot.

"We've still got a few minutes, Dad."

"Naw. It's light enough. It must be time."

Moments later Dad stands and swings on a black that glides in over our right shoulders. He fires once, the duck flares off, and the moment is quickly gone.

"Missed 'em." Dad goes to look for his empty shell.

"Let's worry about them later." I'm not sure whether I mean empty cases or the ducks. It's still five minutes before legal shooting time.

All around the marsh other duck hunters, patient until now, are fingering their shotguns' safeties, muttering, "If that guy's gonna start, I'm starting too." Fifteen seconds have not elapsed when three distant shots thud out. A miss, for sure. Moments later, a closer single salvo. Then a flurry of shots in the distance from the bay. It has started.

A pair of blacks pass over, again from behind us. They call a tentative quack. I ease the call to my lips as they bank to the left: "Duck . . . duck . . . duckaduckaduck." They swing around into the wind, losing altitude, sideslipping toward the rig. Dad stands and shoots, a bit early, but the lead bird falls cleanly beyond the rig. He fires after the climbing second bird but only hurries him on his way.

I lead Win to the edge, away from the tangle of decoy cords, and send her off. Mostly she is here to find cripples that fall in the marsh grass. Her water retrieves are not the extravaganza of a Lab's, but the job gets done. When the weather turns bitter, I leave her home in deference to her spaniel's coat. As I field-dress the duck, Win waits patiently for the liver and heart. The ritual never changes.

"How come you didn't shoot?" Dad asks.

"I told you, but you didn't believe me: This is teal day for me."

"I didn't think *that* would last past the first pair of blacks that decoyed."

On the ride down I had told Dad that he could take all the blacks on both our limits, and I would concentrate on teal. This was the last day of the ten-day bonus season, which could stretch our bag. I like teal because they're excellent on the table, but mostly because they're so much fun to shoot at.

It is not cold, at least not extremely so. But the wind and rain of the fall's first northeaster combine to make it a dirty day for anyone who might be ill equipped. The wind shifts around ninety degrees, and I wade out and move the spread accordingly.

After watching the deliberate maneuvers of blacks throughout the early morning, I react a half-step behind the acrobatic flight of the morning's first flock of teal: They swing by the decoys, and though the shot is an easy one, I cannot swing fast enough for an effective second shot. Only one duck hits the water. The teal flock circles the pothole area, then comes back for another run at our rig. The same shot gets the same result, but this time Dad also takes a bird.

The morning is made of pockets of fast action immediately after a downpour, spaced out by longer periods of empty skies. Waterfowling is mostly waiting. We share a wet Nestle bar and finish the last of the coffee, also diluted with raindrops. But mostly we wait. The rig comes under close scrutiny by its creators during these times: This decoy has a nice profile, and that one floats well, but that bird could use some more ballast. Nearly every improvement made to the various decoy rigs has come about through observations made while waiting.

Teal continue to buzz our salt ponds, but they seldom offer us the luxury of advance notice. They seem to pop up from the horizon, already in range. The magnum gun works against me on these quick shots, and after each miss I ask myself why I brought it if I intended to concentrate on teal? I feel the goose loads in the pocket of my waders and know the answer.

I return from a check on the boat moorings: The tide is running in and is just a couple feet from the top of the bank. The tide table says it won't crest for another ninety minutes. No doubt about it, the marsh will flood over. We have another hour at the most.

Dad sees them first. They are over the dunes, coming in off the ocean almost directly behind us. For a moment I'm not sure. They mill about like sea gulls. Then they group up and begin to fly across the wind in the general direction of our potholes. We haven't seen a single goose since before dawn. Wanting to believe has tricked me before. They could be shang. Or mergansers. There is a moment when they veer to the downwind side, then correct their flight for our pothole. From that moment on I'm sure: They are geese—eleven of them.

I play a few notes on the call: A yodeled "Honk-a-honk . . . honk . . . a-honk." Dad changes loads, and I see the tenseness in his movements. Then he joins the calling.

They continue their labored course across the marsh on a course that will take them along the tidal creek below us. I pump out the gun's three shells into the sod at my feet. Bent over, I try too fast to stuff the long goose loads into the magazine. The second shell hangs up, and there is a moment of panic before I can shuck it out and start over.

Below us they change course, now heading into the wind, past our boat and directly for our rig. From under my hat brim I see the geese fighting the wind, seeking easier going at low altitude, and feel again the adrenalin surge that incoming geese have always brought on. They pass over the far bank of the salt pond two hundred yards away. I hold tightly to Win's collar, but it is an empty gesture: She is also crouched low, her eyes on the geese.

From behind us two coots splash into the rig. They couldn't have timed it better.

The Canadas are out a hundred yards, beginning to look huge, when a thought crosses my mind. I take the call from my lips and am surprised to find that I am out of breath. I whisper to Dad, "Don't shoot the same bird."

Dad nods. He knows.

I switch my hold from Win's collar to Dad's knee.

They cannot glide in the head wind, but their feet dangle and their necks are stretched downward, intent on our goose decoys beyond us. Their reflections pass into the black duck rig.

We rise together. I try to be deliberate with the gun, and hold on the bill of the far left-hand goose. He shudders at my first shot and grabs for air. I lead him and fire again, but he is no longer moving forward and needs no lead. I shoot a third time, below and behind him now as he flares away with the wind. He shudders once more, but glides off on set wings. I watch as he sails down the marsh, back the way he came. His left wing falters a bit, then recovers, then falters again and folds under. He falls.

I won't take my eyes from the spot. I will *not*. Starting out, I call to the dog and see her race ahead. Behind me I hear the clink of the action of Dad's automatic, then a single shot. Finishing a cripple. Good, he finally got one. Good for him.

The marsh is now flooded in spots to just below the grass level, and I slosh along in several inches of unseen water. I step into a hidden cut and stumble, and my hands and the gun go into the water for a moment, but still I won't permit my eyes to leave the place where the goose fell. But as I go farther out, the "spot" becomes a vast expanse. There are sheets of water here I hadn't seen from the rig, and the sameness of the landscape begins to cause doubts: Have I gone too far? Was it beyond this little pothole? "Dead bird, Win. Find dead." She looks back at me, and I wave her toward some tall grass. There is water splashing under her step. My doubts continue, and I am about to wave her to the rear when she goes on point. I whistle her ahead, and in a moment she emerges from the tall grass, backing out, dragging the goose by its neck.

For the first time I turn and wave at Dad. He is standing, watching me. I point to Win, but there is three hundred yards of marsh grass between us, and he shrugs. I go to Win and lift the goose high. He waves back.

"Good girl, Win." I scratch her behind her ears, and she senses my exhilaration, for she runs a couple of tight circles around me as I start back.

Dad's goose is floating behind the black duck rig with the wind pushing it along. With only hip boots on, Dad is pretty much shore-bound. I come up abreast of our gunning point and step into the salt pond to make the retrieve. From the looks of its feet, Dad's goose is a young bird, ideal for roasting.

"Congratulations!" I turn toward shore, holding Dad's goose high.

"The others are over this way." He points toward the goose rig.

Others? *Plural?*

In among the goose decoys, floating belly up, is a second goose. Beyond the rig floats a third. Out of the corner of my eye I watch my father as I wade across the pothole. If he won't smile, neither will I. Win attempts a swimming retrieve of the far bird, but she can't seem to move it through the water. She swims alongside of me as I emerge with forty-odd pounds of geese.

Finally Dad can stand it no longer and breaks into a wide, foolish grin.

"Okay," I say. "Without rubbing it in too hard, tell me about it."

Dad directs my attention to the path of the flock. "They came in so close I figured I had one of the near ones easy, so I pulled on a high one first . . . *Bam!* Down he comes! Then the whole flock flares right up in front of me, so I aimed right at the closest bird in self-defense . . . *Bam!* Down he comes, too! Then they all flared off except one of 'em that tried to climb straight up. I put the gun on him . . . *Bam!* He came down faster than the other two put together."

I shake my head. *"A triple!"*

"I had to finish off one of them. He was swimming away, so I strafed him on the water."

Standing in the rain, he retells the event several times. He is as excited as a boy who has just shot his first pheasant.

My response to each retelling is the same: *"A triple!"* I still can't get over it.

THE FULL-MOON tide continues to rise, and we have water under foot within a half-hour. We stay long enough to take a final black and miss a final teal, then we race the rising water to get our gear back to the boat. After the first trip the water is high enough to float the boat back to the potholes, and we use it to pick up the decoys.

By the time we have finished, we can motor directly across the flooded marsh to the boat ramp. Only the tallest stands of marsh grass remain above water. The northeaster is blowing harder than ever now, and with the shelter of the salt marsh under water, waterfowl are flying inland.

We winch the boat onto the trailer and drive off, leaving the job of stowing the gear until we can find a place to get out of the driving rain. Just beyond the drawbridge is a boarded-up gas station, closed until the summer people return to the coast. I pull the truck under its overhanging roof.

While Dad sets up his stove and makes coffee, I secure the motor and store the decoy sacks and equipment. The camper-back offers a dry place to change clothes and make ourselves presentable enough to sit down at a restaurant before the long haul home.

I have the coffee pot in my hand when a car slows as it passes the gas station. It has a camouflage boat in tow, and one of the faces that gaze out at me belongs to a gray-muzzled old Lab. I wave the coffee pot at them, and they make a U-turn into the drive.

The two hunters get out. I hope they don't have far to travel: They're both soaked and look exhausted. I hand them each a mug and notice that one of them has a definite tremor as I pour the coffee.

"You the fellows that got all the geese?" one of them asks over the rim of his cup.

Dad is just emerging from the truck, freshly shaven, dressed in clean slacks and a sweater, and smelling of Aqua Velva.

"Not me," I reply. *"He's* the one. I was just along as a witness."

Dad grins his broadest grin.

The End

The point is that a cheap suit is still a cheap suit, even if it's made out of hundred dollar bills sewn together.

—Steven Mulak

THE LEAVES were still thick on the aspens, and Stanley was having trouble keeping track of the dog. There were woodcock here—he had taken eleven just yesterday—but he wasn't going to see bird one if he couldn't get that damned puppy under control. Tucking his gun into the crook of his arm, he dug out his whistle and gave a couple of angry blasts.

Nothing.

That dog can't help but hear the whistle, he thought. *She's gonna pay for ignoring me.*

He needed this sort of problem right now like he needed a third nostril: With birds everywhere this could be another golden opportunity to make up the difference for some of the days his limit went unfilled . . . *But where was that damn dog?* Stanley was exasperated. This early in the season it seemed there was always something—if it wasn't the heat or the rain, it was stupid game wardens with nothing better to do than check bird hunters. Not that Stanley ever got caught—he was too smart for that—but aggravations, it seemed, were everywhere. He'd worked with this new puppy through the summer, and she was fine most of the time. But when the birds were thick, she'd get excited and run amuck like she was doing now. Old Spotty used to do that until the day Stanley lost his temper and beat the dog to within an inch of his life. Spotty never ran off again after that.

He heard the puppy's bell off to his right. Deliberately he broke a whippy branch from a birch tree and set off toward the sound. A woodcock bounded up from underfoot, twittering and twisting up through the branches overhead. He tried to get his shotgun to his shoulder but was fouled by some leafy brush. When he yanked at the gun, he only succeeded in snapping back a branch that hit him full in the face and knocked off his hat. The bird vanished beyond the tree-tops. Through clenched teeth he muttered a curse that was a mixture of two contradictory sexual deviations. The sound of the dog's bell came from just beyond an old broken-down stone wall. He picked up the switch with a renewed purpose.

As he stepped across the wall, his foot caught on an unseen twist of rusted barbed wire and pitched him forward. He steeled himself for a bone-jarring fall, but strangely he fell quite painlessly. Stanley scrambled up, still intent on catching the puppy. As he started off, he glanced back to see if anything had fallen from his pockets in the spill.

There, lying face down across the wall, was a man.

"What the hell . . .?" He stepped closer, unsure of what he was seeing. This guy hadn't been there a moment ago. It appeared to be a hunter: The man wore a canvas coat like his own, although it had a jagged tear through the back, and briar-proofs, also like his own. But just why he was sprawled across the wall was unclear. A growing seep of red edged the hole in the man's coat, and wasn't that the butt of a shotgun protruding from under the figure . . .?

He realized then who the man was.

With the toe of his boot he moved the man's hat so he could see the face. His suspicions were confirmed: It was himself.

"I must be crazy," he muttered. He stood listening to his own thoughts for a moment, then breathed out a nervous sigh and sat down on the wall. He couldn't take his eyes from the figure—it appeared he'd fallen on his gun and blown a hole through his chest. But it couldn't be . . . He shook his head. "I guess this is it," he concluded out loud. "I must actually be wack-o. Funny, I don't remember going bananas . . . But, then again, if I am insane, what do I know?"

His puppy came in, tail between her legs. She approached the prone figure, head down, expecting a whipping. He whistled to her, but wasn't heard. "C'mere, Belle." For a moment the dog looked at him, but her eyes were focused beyond, searching for something unseen. "Belle. C'mere, girl." The dog backed up, hackles raised, then lifted her head in a howl. He got up and approached the dog, but Belle turned and ran off.

So much for man's best friend, he thought. *The dumb dog is acting like she's seen a ghost.*

He pondered the idea for a moment. *Is that it? Am I to be the ghost of Tripwire Covert?* He returned and sat next to himself. Crazy or not, things appeared pretty real; a genuine-looking puddle of blood had formed and was dripping from one of the rocks under the body, already attracting a few equally real-looking flies that buzzed around, and the smell of burned gunpowder was pungent in the air. He didn't feel insane—not that he expected that nuts actually felt crazy, either. But he reluctantly admitted to himself that there was more than an outside chance he was actually . . . dead.

Dead, huh? Hmm.

The end.

He hadn't really expected it this soon. He remembered grumbling about the extra charges for the accidental death benefit on his life insurance. Hmm. And just last summer his agent had talked him into mortgage insurance. For that matter, the company had insurance on his loan at work too. "Hey, all right!" He smacked his fist into his open palm. "For once I'm gonna make out like a bandit!" But his grin faded. "Of course, if I'm really dead . . ."

He heard someone coming through the woods. Whoever it was drew closer and walked directly to where Stanley sat on the stone wall. The man was definitely not a hunter—he carried a briefcase and had on a pinstriped business suit, wing-tip shoes, and a Hawaiian shirt that seemed incongruous with his otherwise somber attire. He withdrew a notepad from the pocket of his suitcoat.

"Stanley John Marinski?"

"It's Stanley J. Martin now. I had it changed a few years back."

"Stanley John Marinski, nevertheless. I represent the Eternal Afterlife Corporation and am here to escort you to your final reward, as it were."

"You're an angel?"

The man allowed a momentary look of disgust to cross his face. "We prefer to be referred to as executive afterlife planning coordinators, but yes, I am what you might call . . . an angel."

"So I'm really dead, then."

Expressionless, the angel stared at him for a long moment before shaking his head, then reached into his briefcase and drew out a plain white envelope. The initials S. J. M. were scribbled in one corner. "Mister Marinski, in this envelope are our plans for your future time here in eternity. While your demise was rather sudden, we are eternally vigilant here at E.A.C. and maintain a continually updated list of our prospective clients." The spiel seemed recited by rote. The angel tore open the envelope and examined the note inside with all the interest of someone glancing at the contents of a handkerchief into which he had just blown his nose.

"Wuzzit say?" Stanley asked.

The memorized statements continued. "E.A.C. is pleased to announce that you have been awarded our plan 'J' with options three, four, and seven."

Stanley held his breath for a moment. "Okay. Lay it on me: What does *that* mean?"

"In brief, it means that your wishes have come true."

Stanley blinked.

The angel took his arm and led him away from where the motionless body lay draped over the wall. As they walked, the angel referred to his notepad. "You have often wished for a perfect dog? You are to have one . . ."

"Really?"

An English pointer appeared, white with unusual black markings, and walked at the angel's side. Stanley noticed that the dog marched in step, almost military fashion; left . . . left . . . left-right-left . . .

"The endless season you frequently wished for?"

Stanley shook his head bashfully. "Yeah, but I never paid no mind to seasons and such . . ."

"An endless season is also yours: Here at E.A.C.'s hunting grounds, there is no closed season. And best of all, Mister Marinski, the wish you often made for unlimited shooting is also true: There are no bag limits."

Okay, so what's the catch? thought Stanley. *This sounds too good to be true. Either there ain't any birds, or I've got to use a .22 short rifle on them* . . .

"Nothing of the sort, Mister Marinski."

Holy shit! He can read my mind! Stanley thought. *I mean—Holy smokes!*

"Certainly." The angel did not even glance at Stanley, but the pointer seemed to scowl up at him. "We have arranged a rather fine gun for you to use." He handed Stanley a 20-gauge side-by-side.

It was indeed a fine gun, the sort he had always wished he could afford. The walnut was well figured, the checkering clean, the engraving immaculate. Stanley took a pair of shells from his coat pocket, and when he closed the action on them, the crisp solid click said "quality" with a capital Q. *There's the rub,* he thought. *Ammo. All they're gonna give me for the rest of time is what's in my jacket.*

"Yes," the angel answered his thought. "But that will hardly be the problem it at first appears. Please look in your pocket."

Both empty shell loops were now full again. Stanley smiled.

As they walked, the cover became unfamiliar. They stepped across a small stream and came to a vista that looked out across acres of pasturelands, some overgrown to birch and popple, others laced with alder-lined brooklets. There were abandoned orchards and little tag swamps, and other than a few tumble-down fences and stone walls, the cover stretched to the horizon without any signs of people: There wasn't a house or a paved road in sight. Here and there a tree colored the scene with its autumn foliage, but most were bare. It seemed to be early November and looked to Stanley to be a woodcock hunter's paradise.

"Here we are," spoke the angel. "There is an abundance of some sort of little bird for you to shoot . . ."

"Woodcock?" Stanley crossed his fingers.

The angel referred to his notepad. "Yes, woodcocks." From his briefcase he withdrew a small box with a single pushbutton on its face. "This is a call box, Mister Marinski." He handed the box to Stanley. "If you should find you require my assistance for any reason, you need only push this button."

Stanley took his eyes from the vista for the first time and glanced at the box. "You say this place goes on forever and is full of birds, that I've got full shell loops for the rest of time, and there ain't any limits?" He smiled. "Why should I need to contact *you?*"

The angel paused, fingering the bottom point of a gold star pin on his lapel. "Something might be in need of . . . adjustment." He turned to leave.

"Say, what's the dog's name?" Stanley called after him.

"*Dyabel.*"

Strange name for a dog, he thought. *It almost sounds Polish.* "Well, we'll get along just fine, won't we, fella . . ." He reached out to pet the pointer, but instead the dog bit him on the meat part of the hand. Stanley jumped back. The skin was not broken. Although he had never owned one, he'd always heard pointers were feisty. The dog stood glaring at Stanley. "C'mon, fella." He started down the hill toward the endless covert. The dog accompanied him, not quite at heel.

Oh boy, he thought. *Heaven! I never figured I'd make it, and I certainly didn't think it'd be like this. I don't know what I expected, really—maybe that I could hunt with Spotty again, like in 'The Road to Tinkhamtown'.* He flexed his hand, examining the bite. *No complaints, mind you, but I figured it'd be a place where I could smoke Camels again without rotting out my lungs, and put salt on my eggs without worrying about cholesterol or hardening of the arteries . . . maybe a chance to find out what happens to all those partridge that seem to vanish from the face of the earth after I flush them once . . . Ah, and Cynthia Murphy—how many times have I wondered what she would have been like . . . Or what if I'd gone to Saint Mike's instead of into the navy?* His thoughts ran to the thousands of other questions for which only heaven could hold answers. *Yes indeed, I'll have some questions for that angel when I see him again. But first I'll get some shooting in—maybe a few hundred years or so.* Stanley chuckled to himself. Even his hand felt better.

The pointer charged ahead as they entered the first stand of popple. The dog was lovely to watch: efficient and graceful, casting thirty yards to either side of him in a series of figure 8s. They hadn't gone a hundred yards when the pointer struck scent and slid into a classic point.

Stanley shook his head in amazement: He had never seen anything quite so pretty. He stepped in front of the dog, and a woodcock took flight into the branches above. The double swung effortlessly, and the bird fell at his shot.

He was about halfway to the spot where the bird had come down when he realized that the dog was still standing as if on point. He had never known a dog that was actually steady to wing and shot, but he was seeing one now. He spoke almost apologetically: "Oh, okay . . . Go fetch, fella." The pointer dashed out and brought in the bird. Stanley was impressed. "I think I'm going to like this."

As with every other woodcock he had ever shot in life, he turned the bird over in his hand to see if it had a leg band. This one had one. "Look at this!" he spoke aloud. "I've been waiting all my life to shoot a banded bird." He paused, listening to his own words. "Longer, I guess." He looked closely at the tiny leg band. It read "E.A.C. game farm." *A stocked bird! How tacky.* But Stanley was euphoric, and neither biting bird dogs nor stocked woodcock could dampen his spirits.

Throughout the day, as he walked from one point to the next, he noticed that all of the little unpleasantries of hunting had been removed. What remained of the autumn foliage was pretty but obstructed no shots; no branches swatted him as he moved through the woods, even in the thick stuff; all the birds were sitting just right (even the three partridge the dog had pointed); and surprisingly he hadn't missed a shot. Even his bootlaces were staying tied. When his foot slipped off a rock while crossing a brook and he went in up to his knee, he scrambled out, cursing. He expected a bootful of water, but when he felt his socks, they weren't even damp. *Looks like they've thought of everything,* he thought to himself. *What a pleasure this is—it's almost like heaven.* He chuckled at his own joke.

I guess I wasn't as bad a guy as I thought, he reflected. *I always said you gotta look out for yourself, 'cause nobody else is gonna. It looks like all that crap about givin' your money away and that stupid Golden Rule business is for suckers. Ha. I always knew it. And those Nature-fakers with their game laws must have been way out of line too. Glad I never paid much attention to that sort of thing.* He nodded his head self-righteously. *Yeah, I always played it 'first come, first served,' I guess I was right. Why else would I be in heaven?*

The pointer continued to hunt flawlessly and was a joy to watch. When Stanley made another attempt to pet the dog, the pointer backed away growling, baring his teeth. He was ten times the dog Spotty had ever been, but still in all it would be nice to have the old Brit back again, working the cover in his pokey sort of way, bumping a bird as often as he pointed one. *I'll have to ask the angel about that*, he thought, *right after I light up my first Camel.*

The next shot was a double, with woodcock going out in opposite directions. He dropped the left bird easily, but his barrels caught on a branch as he swung to the right, and when the gun went off, the shot was behind the bird. But the woodcock took an abrupt turn in flight, as they sometimes do, and was crossing back when the pattern caught him in a puff of feathers.

"Now ain't that a piece of luck!" Stanley grinned as the pointer delivered the bird to his hand.

Within the hour, the same thing happened again. Stanley became suspicious. On the next shot, he deliberately aimed above the crossing bird, and sure enough, just as he pulled the trigger, the bird climbed and was caught by the shot pattern for his seventeenth straight shot without a miss.

Stanley shook his head in disgust. "That ain't no fun." His elation was quickly evaporating.

They were crossing through some old birches minutes later when the dog stopped in midstride, pointing to his right. As Stanley approached the deadfall that the dog indicated, a grouse ran out from under the stump and took flight straight away from him. The shot was an easy one, but Stanley pointed the gun back over his shoulder and fired. Very quickly the grouse turned and flew 180 degrees to the rear and managed to get hit. Eighteen in a row.

The pointer brought the grouse in, but Stanley turned his back. "*Eat* the damn bird, for all I care." The dog dropped the bird and bit Stanley on the calf. "All right! *All right!* Gimme the bird." Only when he took the grouse and slid it into his gamebag did the pointer cast off through the cover again. "I'm going to have a talk with that angel about you, you S.O.B.!" he yelled after the dog as he bent to massage his leg. "You can't pull this crap with me. You're *through!*"

The dog went on point again, not fifty feet from where Stanley stood shouting. He started forward, then stopped. *This stinks*, he thought. *Taking this many birds ain't much fun if it's legal. I'm a fun kinda guy: I need a limit to break and some rules to ignore.* He looked to where the pointer stood on point. *An' a dog that's having a good time being a dog, not some mechanical game warden.* Stanley turned his back on the dog's point and went to sit on a rock outcropping, tossing the gun down. Fifty feet away the woodcock bounded up in front of the dog, and as the gun struck the ground, it went off. The bird folded, centered by the pattern. Nineteen for nineteen.

"You call this *fun*?" Stanley muttered. "Birds that commit suicide . . . Dogs that got no respect . . ." He dug out the box that the angel had given him and pressed the button with a vengeance. "I'll get Spotty back." The muttering continued. "He never growled at me 'cept once in a while when I'd get drunk an' kick him one. . . ."

The angel's distant voice emitted from the box: "Hello. I'm either not in at the present or cannot come to the phone. At the sound of the tone. . ."

"A damn answering machine!" Stanley shook his head.

". . . please leave your message, and I may or may not get back to you. Beeeeep. . ."

"Angel?" Stanley spoke into the box. "It's me, Stanley Martin. . ."

"Yes?" The angel was suddenly standing next to him.

"Hey, look—I've gotta talk to you." Stanley scrambled to his feet. "Things are almost *too* perfect here. I mean, it's nice and all, but this sort of never-miss shooting and this mechanical dog act ain't what I'm used to. . ."

"Isn't that what you wished for?"

"Yeah, yeah . . . But what'd *I* know?" Stanley waved in dismissal. "I know I never admitted it, but it was nice to miss once in a while—it made the really good shots all the sweeter. And Spotty—he died last year: he ought to be around here somewheres—I'd like to have him back. He wasn't the best dog ever, but I kind of liked him, an' we had fun. Know what I mean?"

"E.A.C. has already approached a Spotty Marinski in regard to the matter. Evidently, Mister Marinski, Mister Spotty did not much care for you during your previous existence: He refused."

"Why that son of a . . ." Stanley caught himself.

The angel stood indifferently. Stanley's voice grew louder and higher as he continued. "Okay, forget Spotty. Look, I'm not going to make believe I enjoyed it, but getting scratched and swatted by briars and branches was a real part of woodcock hunting, too . . . Getting hung up in the brush so you couldn't shoot, and having the little buggers dodge out of your pattern now and then, and getting caught off guard when a partridge goes out . . . Even getting your feet wet makes you appreciate the days when you manage to stay dry."

The angel shrugged. "Plan 'J,' options . . ."

"To *hell* with that!" Stanley nearly shouted. He grabbed the angel's shoulder in desperation. "Look: Somebody made a mistake about me—a *big* mistake. I don't deserve all this. I used to break the law a lot—I mean, *all the time.* It was a hobby with me. And I never had much use for my fellow man. And I used to poach—*really;* trout, birds, deer . . . you name it. All that Christian foolishness about faith, hope, and charity and don't covet your neighbor's wife? Hope I had, but the others? Forget it. I used to covet all the time . . . Does your boss realize all this stuff?"

"E.A.C. is well aware of your mortal performance evaluation scores. So?"

"What do you mean, 'So?' Look, somebody made a mistake about me. *I'm telling you I don't belong here."* He grimaced a moment, then added desperately, "I should be in . . . in the *other* place."

For the first time the angel smiled. He chuckled. His smile broadened into a grin, and his chuckle became a laugh that became a whoop of hilarity that finally doubled him over in a fit of hysterical laughter.

After his desperate plea Stanley was aghast at the angel's reaction. "What's so funny?" he demanded.

It took a moment, but the angel controlled his laughter long enough to blurt out a reply: "This *is* the other place." The whoops of laughter resumed.

Stanley turned his back on the angel. Beyond a deadfall, twenty yards away, the pointer stood on a classic point, head high, nostrils flared, tail nearly straight up, one foot just off the ground. The sight made Stanley sick to his stomach.

Suzie

AN OLD yellowed document came into my hands the other day. It states that an English setter female named Lyndon's Princess Susan was whelped April 2, 1949. The pedigree shows that she had three lines to Sport's Peerless and that fourteen of her ancestors were champions.

Suzie, I remember you.

We had a springer before Suzie, but I have only a few vague childhood memories of that black-and-white puppy, the most vivid of which involve his dying of distemper. So my father looked for a replacement to help heal the hurt of a family who had lost a dog they had just gotten used to loving. Somebody at work knew of a somebody who was getting rid of a setter. She had spent her life in a kennel as an unsuccessful "shooting dog" on a field trialer's string. Although she had all the credentials, after several seasons of training and campaigning the somebody who owned her decided that she simply wasn't going to make it as a field trial dog. Too soft, he told my father. He had tried to cash in on her pedigree by using her as a brood bitch, but she proved unsuccessful at that, too. There was no reason for the somebody to feed her any longer, but he assured my father she'd make a good hunter and family dog. After all, she was "fully trained." Even more alluring to my father, whose previous dogs had all been of dubious lineage, she possessed the ultimate status symbol—she had papers.

So Suzie came into our lives. She wasn't a "boy's dog," like Lassie or Ol' Yeller, but when she wasn't hunting with Dad, she belonged to my brothers and me. She pulled a sled out in the winter street while I pretended I was Sergeant Preston, and she loved to come to the park with us in the summer, more to cold-nose-it with the neighborhood mongrels than out of any protective instinct for her charges. She lived in the house with our family, and spent her evenings in the den by the TV. On hot summer nights she would sneak into the bathroom and curl up next to the cool porcelain of the toilet bowl. After five years in a kennel life at our house must have seemed like heaven. Except during thunderstorms. Although she was never gun shy, I've never known another creature to be more afraid of thunder, and there was no calming her when lightning split the clouds open.

As a kid, I was in no position to judge her hunting abilities. My dad was a kind and generous man but never pretended to be a trainer of bird dogs, at least not to the extent that he could undo the mistakes of another man. He took in a dog that had spent her life with any number of professional trainers, all shaping her for one purpose— winning field trials. Her inability to respond to the often hard-handed production line methods of the pros was the reason she became available. Now when she tried to do right by her old discipline, she found that my father, a pheasant hunter, wanted something entirely different from her. I never knew Dad to actually hit either dog or boy, but he could deliver a blistering "verbal correction" while holding onto a dog collar (or in my own case, an ear) that left no doubt as to his displeasure. Whenever Suzie would decide that the time had come to tear up the back course, she would soon after discover my father holding onto her collar, slightly out of breath and shouting something new to her: *"Hunt close!"*

And in her confusion, Suzie would cry.

Her crying was the one most exemplary character trait I remember about her. She would cry when other dogs would have barked; at the door to be let out, and again on the other side to be let back in again. She would cry while her food was being prepared and cry when she was put into the cellar for the night. She cried with excitement in the car on the way to go hunting, and then cry again at the end of the day. She would cry in her sleep, and most unfathomable to a little boy, she would cry when I'd pet her.

I didn't then understand what she'd been through. In my memory I can see a cool blue afternoon on the Agawam meadows through the eyes of a boy who is shorter than the dried-up milkweed and goldenrod around him. I can see my father coming out of the standing corn without the pheasant he and Suzie went in to retrieve. We wait a while for the dog to return, then start walking down the farm road, pausing every few steps to call for her. We finally spot her coming along the road behind us. She is covered with swamp muck and is carrying a long-tailed rooster. Dad kneels to accept the bird from her, and while he tells her what a good girl she is, he reaches out to pat her head. Suzie pulls away from his hand, crying.

I recall Dad telling a friend that he never once called her in when she didn't expect a whipping. Though he never laid a hand on her, she was that way as long as she lived. Significantly, my father never again owned a dog that he did not start himself from a puppy.

ALTHOUGH SHE was ever welcome in the house, Suzie slept in the cellar and was sent to "go lay down" in the basement whenever she got in the way of goings-on, as a fifty-pound dog will often do in a tiny house.

It was Thanksgiving. The refrigerator was already full to overflowing, so amidst a barrage of warnings to be careful, I carried four oven-hot lemon meringue pies down the cellar stairs and set them, as instructed, on the concrete floor to cool. Two hours before dinner, my aunts began to crowd in. Each new arrival that came through the door was greeted by Suzie's cold nose against a nylon-stockinged leg. In near-automatic reaction, my mother collared Suzie and with a practiced ease led her to the cellar door, never interrupting the stream of conversation she was carrying on with her sisters.

A few minutes later I happened to be looking directly at my mother when she did a classic double-take, complete in every detail save the light bulb going on over her head. A small scream was screamed and the cellar door hurriedly flung open. Suzie was on the top step. Bits of meringue still clung to the parts of her whiskers and eyebrows her tongue couldn't reach. She stood around the kitchen, tongue busy, while my mother hustled Dad into the room to see what "his dog" had done. Long after it stopped being a joke, Suzie continued to happily lick her face, for once ignoring the scolding she was getting. My grandmother and I thought the whole thing was quite funny, although, with the dog, we were a minority of three. I don't recall how things turned out that Thanksgiving, but knowing my mother's penchant for holiday desserts, I'm sure there were several other choices on the menu. But in my fondest memories of her, I can still see Suzie of the soft brown eyes with persistent bits of meringue clinging to the fur on her face.

SHE LIVED her days in our suburban back yard, fenced in to become a sixty-by-forty-foot kennel which she shared with the rest of the family. Although she tolerated my mother's laundry hanging at one end of her domain, she sabotaged any attempt by my father to grow shrubs in the yard, and eventually chewed the life out of any rose or lilac planted along the fence. And although she was always gentle with people, she harbored a deep hate for the neighborhood cats that ventured along the fence. Other dogs simply detest cats. Suzie became a *legend* because of her animosity toward them.

We were stripping tobacco at my uncle's one fall evening when her opportunity for fame arose. Tobacco stripping is the process of removing the cured leaves from the stems on which they have been hanging. It's tedious work, and the atmosphere is not unlike a masculine version of a ladies' quilting bee, except that it takes place in a tobacco barn under the harsh glow of a Coleman lantern, and the conversation is punctuated by the frequent stomping of cold feet on the dirt floor. One of my uncles was running on about his tough old farm cat, telling everyone who would listen how it had run off a stray mongrel just that morning, and how it would outsmart any dog it couldn't beat in a stand-up fight. To be sure, the cat could have passed for a lynx if it wasn't for his long tail. He was a big, *big* tom who stared out at the world through squinted eyes and would permit no little boys within rock-throwing distance of him.

In reply my father casually mentioned that he happened to own a dog that didn't fool around much with cats. She just killed 'em. Now, I myself had never seen Suzie actually *catch* a cat, but I had seen her sprint the length of the yard after them, and my imagination was vivid enough to fill in the blanks each time she nearly nabbed one. I promptly agreed with Dad.

The conversation grew louder, and though the men never lost the laughter from their voices, there was a determined look on my father's face when he left the barn and drove off into the night in our old Plymouth. It must have all been agreed upon before Dad left, because there was hardly a word spoken when he returned with Suzie a half-hour later. The lantern was moved to an open spot. My uncle placed his cat down on the dirt floor, and Dad let go of Suzie's collar.

She approached the cat with raised hackles. The cat arched its back and hissed wickedly. Most dogs will circle, not sure of what to do and offering the cat a chance to run so they can chase it. Suzie didn't feint or circle. She walked close to the cat, paused for just an instant, then lunged and clamped onto the tom with an animal quickness I hadn't realized she possessed. She shook him twice, wildly, then gave the cat a deliberate snap and threw him to the ground. She had broken the cat's neck, but had only thrown him down to get a better grip, for now she picked up the lifeless tom and continued to shake him—perhaps as a surrogate for all the others that had escaped over the backyard fence.

My uncles found something interesting in the dirt they scraped with their boots while Dad collared Suzie and brought her out to the car. When he returned, several pieces of folding money changed hands, and afterward only Dad was smiling. In the entire gathering of perhaps a dozen men, only my father had thought gentle Suzie was a match for the farm cat. The event became a legend: When Floyd Patterson knocked out Ingemar Johansson in the first minute of what was supposed to be the heavyweight fight of the century, Dad pronounced it "just like Suzie and the cat." If in my fondest memories of her I see meringue on Suzie's whiskers, I'm sure my father conjures up an image of her as the self-satisfied dog he permitted, for once, to sit on the front seat of the Plymouth as we drove home that night.

A DOG'S LIFE is short by any measure, and Suzie had already spent half her allotted years when she came to us. Arthritis shortened her life. Dad took her to the vet's one time and didn't bring her back home again.

But I still see her.

At field trials there is always an abundance of misfit dogs; people-loving dogs obviously out of place on the string of a professional trainer, and sensitive dogs that will never be successful because they need a larger amount of love than their impersonal handlers can afford to give. There are easy-going dogs being pushed to run like race horses, and wound-up dogs that want nothing more than to run and hunt, but mostly just to *run*. No, there is never any lack of misfits, being hacked down by men determined to make walking gun dogs out of them.

She's there. Sometimes she even looks the part: There are always a few feathery square-muzzled English setters at any field trial, some without a single patch of solid color in their ticking. I am a chronic petter of all dogs. Saying hello by scratching a dog's ears is something of a compulsion with me. But I am attracted to misfit bird dogs for other reasons too—I look hard, and in their eyes I can often see Suzie looking back at me, and in my imagination I can sometimes see meringue on their whiskers.

The Streak

If the only satisfaction to be derived from the sport lay in killing birds, I would have quit the game long since.

—Burton Spiller

It was a big male grouse at the Indian Oven Covert that started it all: I was following an old pasture wall back toward the truck after chasing a flight of woodcock around some alder runs, and the breeze carried the faint cider smell of windfalls as I approached a line of broken-down apple trees. Hazel's bell indicated she was crossing up out of the junipers below me. The grouse must have been feeding on those windfalls and thought himself too far from suitable cover, because he blasted out of the blackberry tangles beneath the trees at my setter's approach, retreating back over my left shoulder. Evidently he hadn't heard I'd been practicing that particular shot. The dog made a running retrieve, and when I posed her on the wall with the grouse that November afternoon, the picture was pretty enough to make the cover of *Sports Afield*.

That started the streak—seven cock grouse with seven shots. *Big deal*, I thought I heard you say. For me it was. Understand that a single grouse riding in my game bag is a genuine thrill that I've never quite gotten used to, and in twenty years of grouse hunting I've had streaks where I've *missed* seven in a row, but never anything quite like this. Let me tell you about it:

The fourth of November was a gray and overcast day. I went to a place called the Junkyard to hunt woodcock. They normally spend most of the daylight hours sleeping, and because of that they usually hold well for even an inexperienced pointing dog. But when they're not catching Zs, they feed by wandering around, probing for worms. The scent trail of one of these meandering woodcock is such that a hunter might think his dog was following a running bird. When a whole flight has shifted its routine and feeds during daylight hours, (most likely because they've just flown in the previous night) even a normally staunch pointing dog can look bad.

At the Junkyard we got into an actively feeding flight, and Hazel was making a dozen false points for every bird she produced. As a result, I didn't think much of it when one of her walking points led away from the brook we had been following. When the understory petered out, a grouse flushed ahead of her and tried to double back along the edge of the cover, presenting a retreat shot off my right shoulder. I've missed that shot often enough over the years to know how *not* to do it by now, but I can still miss it as often as not. This time I didn't. A second bird was out beyond the first, unnoticed until after I had pulled the trigger. He broke the skyline flying a parallel course to his partner, and I took him with the tight barrel. It happened so quickly that I stood for a moment wondering if I had imagined it all: There were no feathers in the air, no witnesses, only the two empties and a wisp of smoke coming from the open barrels. Then Hazel brought in the first of the pair, and I knew it was all reality.

It was my first-ever grouse double. Honest-to-goodness chances to take a pair of grouse in the air at the same time are once-per-season opportunities—*if* you're lucky. One year, when I was *really* lucky, I had three separate chances at legitimate grouse doubles, but it didn't matter: I missed them all. So understand that having Hazel retrieve *two* cock grouse to me on that cloudy dark morning was not the sort of thing I took lightly. I was dumbfounded. It was a feeling that was to last all through the week. I hung the birds in a twisted little hawthorn tree and posed Hazel next to them for a portrait, then I sat on the tailgate of the truck, stretching out my coffee break in the hopes that someone would drive by and ask how the hunting was. No one did.

On the way home I got off the turnpike in West Springfield and stopped at a liquor supermarket where they have virtually everything. I knew what I wanted. It was five o'clock, and in my Bean boots and tattered canvas shirt, I must have looked to the other customers like the guy who mowed the lawn stopping in for his paycheck. But I didn't care—the only choice I had to make was between the *Blanc-de-noirs* and the *Brut*.

Years ago when my daughters used to come home from kindergarten and hold a crayon drawing up for inspection, my wife would say in her best Jane Wyman voice, "Why, that's very nice." There was a time her attitude toward my shooting exploits was pretty much the same, but with time that changed, and I'm now blessed with a wife who can recognize the importance of my accomplishments. So I was looking forward to sharing my excitement with her, and I came through the door with the pair of grouse in one hand and the bottle of Piper Sonoma in the other: "Look, Honey—after all these years I finally shot a double on grouse—*a double!*"

She was peeling vegetables for supper and barely turned away from the sink. "Why, that's very nice," she said. Then, after a pause, Jane Wyman asked, "What's the champagne for?"

TWO DAYS LATER I was back out again, hunting woodcock in the rain on an overgrown farm in Bondsville. I named the covert after a hunter I met here one day a few years back: After we exchanged hello's, I asked him how he was doing. "Wonderful!" he replied; then, almost under his breath, he asked if I knew what the limit was on quail. Now, quail are not legal game birds in my end of the state for the same reason there is no open season on ostriches and flamingos—there aren't a whole lot of them running around wild. He showed me the four quail he had taken: They had long bills and funny feet and looked a lot like woodcock to me, but the other hunter insisted he *knew* woodcock, and these weren't them. That was okay by me—my father advised me long ago about not arguing with folks when they're carrying loaded guns. So I named the place for that hunter, and it's been "Quailshooter's" ever since. (One of these days I'm going to do a painting that'll clear up once and for all what those "things" are. It will be along the lines of so many I've seen of a hunter's daily kill hanging on a cottage door—but it will be entitled, "Woodcock, Woodchuck, Woodpecker, Wooden pecker, Wood duck, and Wooden duck." With my luck, it'll be a big hit, but they'll misspell the title as well as my last name, and it will only add to the confusion.)

At Quailshooter's Hazel worked along the edge of the cover with her head high. Where a finger of aspens hooked out into a field she doubled back, and when she pointed, it was more tentative than solid. With Hazel every point imparts its own meaning, and I hurried ahead, knowing that this bird could go at any moment. I stopped when a grouse took wing from the far end of the run, then, in the moment before I could let my guard down, a second bird jumped out much closer to me. For once I held above a rising bird and put him down—another male, this one with a tail edged in chocolate rather than black and smaller than either of Monday's birds.

His far-flushing partner had appeared to slant behind the old potato storage barn beyond the finger of popples. Boarded up and weather-beaten, the barn squatted in the tall weeds with its back to the woods, looking like something from a child's nightmare. I sat for five minutes beneath its overhang, giving the flown grouse time to settle down and forget about the hunter that was after him. Once I would have timed myself by smoking a cigarette, but Camels and I have long since parted company. Instead I dressed out the bird in my gamebag.

When we started off again, Hazel slashed through the cover behind the barn, unaware that the grouse was near. She was accelerating out of a turn when the scent hit her, and the beautiful clumsiness of her skidding point resembled the unfolding of an uncooperative deck chair. In that instant she had the bird pinned. It was the sort of point I wait all year to see, and I was still smiling when I made the flush. The shot was quick and clean, and Hazel almost danced as she brought the bird to me. It's glorious each time I take a grouse, but some occasions are more so than others. Hazel's point made this one extra-special.

"Not bad—two for two," I muttered. It was at this juncture that I realized I had a streak going. Listening to my own thoughts, I counted back: There was the double on Monday, and the bird at Indian Oven before that—all unpunctuated by any misses in between. Unquestionably there is an element of luck involved in every grouse shot (or in hitting *anything* with a shotgun, for that matter), but this seemed uncanny: I'm just not that consistent of a wingshot—five in a row was way over my head. My kid brother once went an entire season in Pennsylvania without missing a pheasant—he was something like fourteen for fourteen. But grouse shooting is altogether different: It's more than just bird shooting with trees thrown in. As in baseball, most of us bat around .250, and three out of ten will get you into the majors. And five for five is just plain lucky.

When I got back home, there was a note waiting for me: Susan was shopping and would I please remember to turn on the oven at four o'clock, and P.S., John had called to say there was a flight of woodcock in Compass Covert. Great—here was a chance to give the puppy some work on birds. Zelda was five months old then, and just beginning to suspect that there was more to going afield than running amuck and chasing sparrows around the woods. I left Hazel at home and put the puppy in the truck and even remembered to leave a note for my daughters, reminding them to turn the oven on when they came in from soccer practice.

Whether or not the puppy appreciated her lessons, I certainly got some mileage out of the opportunity. She got hauled in by her check cord when she ran up the first three or four woodcock, and I managed to steady her up on several others. I actually shot *at* a couple, although *hitting* woodcock using just one hand while holding a straining puppy's collar in the other is a low-percentage endeavor.

I was watching my steps, trying to avoid accidently stepping on Zelda's check cord, when a grouse flushed twenty-five yards away from the end of a viburnum run. The bird quartered uphill just above the tops of the bushes—an easy shot, but there was a moment's hesitation until I was sure of the puppy's location. That little hitch and the fact that I was using light woodcock loads added up to a down-but-not-out bird. He fell just beyond a little oak tree that still clung to its leaves.

Puppy or not, Zelda was all I had available at the moment, and I brought her to the leafy oak and told her to "find dead!" I stepped as I waved her ahead, and as I did, my foot came down on the grouse. Not near it—*on* it. It is difficult to do something and not write down a better version, but there can be no exaggeration to that event—I actually stepped on the bird. Simple pleasures can be ruined by examining them too closely. I put the bird in my gamebag and tried not to think of what the odds were of finding a crippled bird in the thick stuff without a trained dog, let alone actually stepping on his back. A million to one seems like a conservative estimate. The bird was yet another cock, and his turned out to be the biggest tail of the season. A simple pleasure—and an amazing piece of luck.

As I DROVE home along School Street, the road curved and headed due west. The day had cleared off, and the lavender afterglow of the cloudless sunset illuminated all I saw through the windshield. At the top of my field of vision something caught my eye as it flew past: It was a woodcock, buzzing along in the dusk toward the woods looming darkly beyond the field to the left. I pulled the truck to the roadside and watched until the dusk swallowed him. With my hand on the gearshift I sat for a long moment, looking out after the bird. The evening star winked in the twilight just above the thin sickle of the moon. In autumn I don't bother making wishes—on days like this I know I'm living out what I'd be wishing for, although I often allow my sense of time to spoil my pleasure: Too often I think in terms of "just eleven days of the season left." I wish I could be more like my dogs and believe that autumn would last forever—or at least not worry about the fact that it won't.

ON THURSDAY night my friend Mike drove down from Vermont. I sometimes do some early season woodcock hunting with him in the Northeast Kingdom, and in return he comes to Massachusetts to shoot pheasants. My dogs like Mike and always seem to do a superior job when he's around. I wish he'd visit more often.

The next day was the first wool-shirt day of the autumn. Win was in her last season but showed off her years of experience when she outwitted a rooster behind an old farm in Monson. I flushed the bird for Mike. In all of bird hunting there is only one thing more glorious than a cock pheasant's rise into the blue November sky over a good dog's point, and that one thing is to be able to produce that event for someone who appreciates it. Mike did, and wasn't afraid to say so.

The old pasture in Monson is a tangle of juniper and low bush blueberries growing among a typical New England boulder collection. Bovinettes of dairy cows appeared unexpectedly in odd places. With the rooster riding in the game pocket of Mike's vest, we looked for woodcock along a brook valley where I had found a flight a week before.

Instead we found a continuation of my streak. Win worked up a little side valley and back out again but could locate only the bird's scent. I believe some birds, when they realize a scenting animal is following them, will fly a short distance to break their trail and then wait in hiding nearby so that they can resume feeding when the danger has passed. I've witnessed it a few times, and I feel sure it must happen to bird dogs more frequently than we nonscenting predators will ever realize. The grouse that gave Win the slip made the unlucky decision to hide in a clump of sorrel overlooking the valley. I, in turn, made the lucky decision to walk through that same sorrel clump as I hurried to catch up with Win. The bird flushed and headed downhill, catching me off-guard for a moment, and although I don't recall it, Mike reports he heard me say a discouraging word just before I shot. His version is that he didn't hear the bird fly but from across the brook saw me fire my gun downhill and thought perhaps I had stepped in one cow flop too many and was opening hostilities against them.

I had mentioned the streak to him, and as Win brought the brown-phase bird in, he asked, "Another male?" It was. "You'd better miss one pretty soon, or you'll be getting so caught up in this 'not-missing' thing that you'll be afraid to shoot—afraid you'll miss, and afraid you *won't*." Mike was joking, but his statement came very close to the truth.

WOODCOCK charm me—there's no other term for it. And in my end of the country the two weeks that include the first ten days of November are what woodcock hunters spend the other 350 days of the year waiting for. All but one of the grouse I've written about here were taken with one-ounce loads of 9s—that should say something about what I was doing in the woods while all this was taking place. It was raining on the eleventh, but I was out, sweating myself wet inside my waterproofs, trying to find "just one more big flight." I once heard an articulate person describe woodcock hunting as a "disproportionate pleasure." When the water starts to work its way down the tops of my boots (a process called "reverse hydropercolation"), I try to focus my attention on that term rather than my empty gamebag.

I was just beginning to get wet when Hazel pointed in some birch scrub. Someday I'm going to discover a way to train a dog to signal to me when she's on point; one wink will mean woodcock, two for a pheasant, and three for a grouse. Hazel has never mastered my signaling technique, and I approached her point thinking "woodcock." It turned out to be a three-winker, and as the grouse thundered through the wet branches, the in-flight impression was that she was a she—it's a matter of proportions: tail to body size. I also observed that I'd used up whatever allotment of luck had been assigned to me, and my shooting had returned to normal: I committed my own personal classic error and failed to hold above the rising bird.

The streak was over. I'm not going to say I was glad, but if you've ever seen that black-and-white press photo of Joe DiMaggio looking emotionally drained and physically exhausted as he sat in the clubhouse with reporters clustered around him on the day his record batting streak ended, you'll understand what I was thinking. Don't get me wrong: I didn't *feel* like Joltin' Joe—I was only glad I *didn't*. Streaks and records and such can easily become so important they distract from the business of enjoying the sport of hunting—the *noncompetitive* sport of hunting. I like hitting birds, but there is a certain laugh-at-yourself sort of enjoyment to be derived from missing, too. It's something you have to permit yourself to do.

I reloaded and started off through the rain toward a spot where I hoped to relocate the hen grouse. I could have had eight in row if I had just blotted out that bird . . . I shouldered my gun and swung through an imaginary riser, but then I laughed out loud—*who's kidding who? I know a .250 hitter when I see one!*

Cycles

When one tugs at a single thing in nature, he finds it is
attached to the rest of the world.

—John Muir

THE MORNING SUNLIGHT slanting through the naked branches could,
without overtaxing my imagination, be a remnant of a morning from
last November: The air is wool-shirt cool, the shadows hold a few
scattered patches of old snow—and the woodcock migration is on.
Almost as if to complete the illusion, my young setter hesitates and
then takes a pair of cautious steps before stopping in a tentative point.
I cross the little brook and hurry to grasp her check cord just as the
twitter of wings breaks her resolve, and her resulting lunge forward
nearly pulls my arm out of its socket. After a moment's struggle I
wrestle the pup back into a pointing posture, command her to Hold,
then walk a few steps and fire the blank pistol into the air. Whatever
intensity she showed on her point is absent, but she stands until I
whistle her on. Some day I might figure out a finesse method of
actually teaching a dog what I want, but until then repetition will have
to do. I open the revolver and dump out the spent blank .22 cases for
the second time this morning.

I reload as I walk on, and my attention is divided between the
display of boundless puppy energy by old Win's replacement and the
resurgence of life that is springtime in New England. We are following
a brook where the emerging fiddleheads are a study in miniaturiza-
tion—each is a full fern leaf, complete in every detail, rolled tight and
only awaiting the unfurling push of life's juices. The first of the marsh
marigolds are in bloom, growing out of the water at the edge of the
brook. The larger blooms are the size of half-dollars. Theirs is the pure
yellow of a child's crayon box, all the brighter for the buttery gloss of
the petals. Willows are everywhere, their gray catkins gone to yellow-
green florets. The liquid call from an unseen redwing blackbird seems
to ride on the sunbeams slanting through the branches. A month ago
the Valentine's Day storm dumped nearly a foot of snow here, yet
today the lowlands are alive once more. I walk on, through what
Hal Borland often referred to as "a quiet miracle."

New smells for the pup are everywhere, and her short attention span works against my efforts to keep her hunting. She chases up a robin, then several more. Robins have been wintering over for the past several years, but I wonder how they've fared the unusually bitter months we've just endured. They are supposed to be a sure sign of spring, but I've always put a lot more stock in the arrival of the first woodcock.

At the bottom of the slope the ground turns swampy, and ahead a green sea of new skunk cabbage leaves promises wet going. I whistle to the pup and direct her uphill toward the birches on our left. As I change directions, a woodcock flushes a few feet in front of me, pretending to be fast, "woodcocking" his way through the dense branches overhead. (The verb could well be a legitimate one: "To dodge by a random series of course changes.") In spring, when the only gun I carry is a blank training pistol, I am continually impressed by the amount of time for a would-be shot that each flush presents the hunter. Admittedly my perspective is different in autumn, but I know I rush far too many opportunities without good reason.

On the leaf mulch where the woodcock had been squatting are several small white puddles, and the pup is about to get called in for a noseful when I notice that she is pointing. The bird flushes before I can get to her, and for a moment it looks as if the pup will not break and chase after the bird. I hold my breath, but the moment ends when the climbing woodcock abruptly elects to sit back down again after flying a scant fifty feet. The coiled spring that is any puppy on point unwinds in a mad rush, and bird and dog disappear downhill into the swamp. Although woodcock reek of scent and hold well for even clumsy points, their propensity for occasional short-hop flights keeps them from being a perfect bird for puppy training. It takes me a full five minutes to whistle the pup back in from the skunk cabbage.

Farther along the birch slope we pass through a little stand of hemlocks. My pulse quickens. On the reverse side of the year I moved a grouse when I came through these same hemlocks, and after I missed him with both barrels, his partners decided to leave—all three of them. There is no logical reason to expect an encore of the incident, but I do, and fight off a twinge of disappointment when only a wood thrush takes flight from the far side of the evergreens. But in the distance I hear the rolling sound of a drumming grouse—one of that same autumn quartet, I hope.

Beneath the birches the blossoms of bloodroot appear like scattered bits of tissue above the forest floor. If one looks for them, the tiny Canada mayflower and Dutchman's breeches are in bloom now too, as is my favorite, the Jack-in-the-pulpit. They take the sun quickly while the woodlands are still bare, and as a result, all are short-lived blossoms, often fading before the plant itself sends up its first leaf. Perhaps it is for this reason that nearly all of the flowers that man has taken into his garden trace their origins to the blossoms of the field rather than the forest. But holding the pure whiteness of a bloodroot flower in my fingers, I can't help but think the horticulturists missed a great deal when they passed up this one.

The puppy is working scent: Her tail bounces with excitement, and her nose is nearly in the dead leaves and bloodroot flowers. I stand on her check cord to stop her, then lift her head so her nose is scenting the air. I've watched as woodcock walk in a seemingly aimless series of circles, hairpins, and figure 8s as they feed: The pattern of scent laid down has to resemble a maze. It must be a natural defense against predators who also hunt with their noses. A trailing dog will have problems with the maze, but a dog that seeks out the scent carried in the air can usually go directly to the bird. The puppy has her head down again. Old Win was a woodcock dog of the first degree, but even she loved to put her nose down and smell those footprints once in a while. I step on the check cord again—when she gets to be as good as Win was, maybe I'll look the other way once in a while, but today she's got to learn the right way. Still, I find as I lift the pup's head once again that I'm using the same gentle touch I needed in training that other woodcock dog a dozen years before.

From far away I hear what seems to be a barking dog. I stop in the next clearing and search the southern sky. At first they seem like an indefinite pencil mark, but as they come closer, I am able to make out individual geese in the wavering line. They are V'ed up, and as they pass overhead, I can see the white chin patches on each bird. I would think they'd want to save their breath, but there is a constant gabble from the flock.

It would be only rational to think of springtime as simply a phase of the year's continuous cycle that the migrating Canadas represent— the year never really ends or begins; it simply changes as one season inexorably becomes the next. But springtime is something that transcends the cold reality of fact and demands the warmth of understanding. In autumn I can tell myself that the year has not really died and count the dormant buds at each branch's end as witnesses to that fact. But spring seems a time for rebirth, a new beginning, and the proof is in the miracle of life's renewal. The miracle goes on all around us, overhead and underfoot, more profound than anything the mind of man has ever dreamed up. Spring is a time for starting over.

The pup has found another woodcock, and this one is more cooperative about holding for her point. I spot the coal-black button of the bird's eye first, then see the rest of the bird hunkered on last fall's now-matted leaves. This is the twentieth woodcock we've found in an outing of little more than an hour, far more than we'd ever find on even the best flight days of autumn.

The springtime migration of woodcock is a huge tsunami compared to the little meandering waves of the fall. The great horde of impatient birds nearly pushes the thaw northward, and doing so, they are prone to disastrous storms like the April blizzard in 1982 which trapped and killed so many woodcock in New England.

My puppy stands firm on this bird, and in answer to my singular command remains unmoving as I cross some unseen boundary and set off the brief flurry of wings. I fire the blank pistol, and the child's squeaky-toy sounds fade away and still the puppy has not moved, although her eyes strain after the bird's flight. As of this moment I own a staunch dog, and will never again quite be able to forgive her breaking point.

Grinning, I kneel on one knee and call her to me. She seems as pleased with herself as I am with her, and she playfully dodges my attempts to pet her. With a clap of my hands I get to my feet and send her ahead.

March woodcocking is proof enough of my belief that if it ever came down to a choice between leaving the dog or the gun at home, there would be no hesitation on the part of most woodcock hunters. Woodcock charm everyone who pursues them, but, more than with any other gamebird, woodcocking without a dog is an exercise in futility: *Dog work* is what woodcock hunting is all about. But a bird dog's life is short by any measure, and dogs, even woodcock dogs of the first degree, have a way of growing old and dying before their human hunting partners are ready to accept those facts. Ahead of me the setter puppy is a white streak through the birches. She'll be a good one—someday. Maybe even every bit as good as Win, who now lives only in my memory.

Spring is indeed the right season for starting over.

'Coon Wars

> This is not to say that wolves are bad people: The entire
> point is they are not people at all. They are wolves.
>
> —Tom McIntyre

FISHING DAYS on the Penobscot always end too quickly. It was September, and although the salmon weren't biting, neither were the bugs. Without bugs I can really enjoy fishing—even without fish.

There is a joyful sort of bone-tiredness that comes of playing hard all day. In that condition an after-supper drink or two or three can have telling effects on the senses. Unaware of the fading twilight, we sat around a driftwood campfire, trading stories with the fellows from the next camp and getting pleasantly lit. When the fire began to fade, the stark blackness of the Maine night made us aware of the hour. We all shuffled around for a minute or two in the darkness, making certain nothing was left out that should have been put away. After checking that the cooler chest lid was firmly fastened and that the rods were on the roof of the car where no one was going to step on them on the way to the john, I retreated into the wall tent and got on with my fumbling attempts to get into my sleeping bag. Cramped quarters and tangled clothes are a tough enough combination, but having paddled at least ten thousand miles that day, all upstream, and then suffered through several refills of Canadian didn't make the session go any more smoothly.

I was drifting toward the Land of Nod when I became aware that all wasn't right in the tent. This was not the normal bickering between my father and Uncle Hank about eating potato chips in the tent or farting or who made the worst coffee. No. Something serious was going on, because my father was putting on his shoes and gathering up a flashlight and a broom. His legs hadn't seen the sun since 1951, and in his baggy boxer shorts he appeared in the night like something that would make the faint of heart scream out loud.

"Wuzzgoin' on?" I blinked back to wakefulness. Next to me my brother was sitting up, watching.

"Dad thinks there's a raccoon raiding our trash."

"So? What's he gonna do with the broom, clean up after him?"

Alan chuckled at that, and after a moment's consideration

shouted to my father, "Hey, Dad—you'd better bring a dustpan too: They're messy buggers." Now I'll admit that on the printed page that might not seem like the wittiest remark ever uttered, but at the time and in our collective condition it struck us both funny and set the tone for the next few minutes.

Outside the beam of Dad's flashlight caught a raccoon. It had knocked over one of the fifty-five–gallon drums that serve as trash cans and was defiantly standing guard over the spilled contents. The 'coon bared his teeth at the flashlight.

"Shine the light on your legs, Dad . . . That'll scare him off."

Our suggestion went ignored. Instead we heard loud sputtering to the effect of: *"Snarl at me, will you . . ."* Dad momentarily blinded the raccoon with the light, then smacked him with the broom and sent him retreating into the darkness.

"Way to go, Dad!" I yelled. "Protect that trash." Alan thought that was hilariously funny, and I seconded his laughter.

In the tent my Uncle Hank had been watching too, and he contributed, "Hey, that's jacklighting."

"Damn right," Dad replied. His flashlight found another 'coon. This one took two smacks before he retreated. Alan took up a rhythm to the tune of "Brazil":

Smack that 'coon—wack your porcupine;
smack that 'coon—wack your porcupine . . .
And I sang:
Raccooooooon . . .
Just let me hit you with my broooooom,
Beneath the light of the old moooooooon,
And don't come back again too soooooon,
Raccoooooon!
(smack that 'coon—wack your porcupine . . .)

"You kids aren't so big you can't *still* get a good swift kick in the ass, you know . . ." In the seventy-odd years' combined experience we had as Dad's kids, we had heard that threat a few times before. It somehow had never struck us quite so funny as it did now. Dad played his light around the campsite. "Hey, there's a whole gang of them out here," he said. The original pair of raccoons had been just the skirmish line for a large-scale raid. Now his flashlight revealed a dozen 'coons advancing on our trash cans.

"Okay," Alan yelled, "here comes the cavalry."

I had no idea what we were going to do, but we both got up and stumbled outside to roust the invaders. Dad held the light while Alan and I mounted a counteroffensive. Our laundry line was handy, so,

God help us, we went after those raccoons with rolled up towels, snapping away and feeling very much like characters from some low-budget comedy. Fully sober, I'm certain that neither of us would have interfered with the raid. As it was, even though they had never been in a locker room towel fight with the brothers Mulak, the raccoon brigade instinctively knew enough to retreat. Nature protects her critters that way.

Right around the time we were regaining our senses, Uncle Hank sprung out into the night like a white streak. His legs had a few years on Dad's, and under ordinary circumstances he and my father would have scared each other. "One of those sons-a-bitches is in the *tent!*" he hollered.

"It's them goddamn potato chips of yours, Hank." Dad never lets up. "I told you before . . ."

In the flashlight's beam a raccoon was seen leaving the tent with a $1.39-size bag of Lay's All-Naturals. Alan yelled after him, "You're gonna get zits eating those things!" and we whooped and laughed over that too, until we couldn't stand up any more.

It was dark, but I don't believe my father nor my Uncle Hank once cracked a smile. My Dad is normally proud of his boys, but now and again there are occasions when he's sure we're throwbacks to my mother's side of the family.

FISHING DAYS on the Penobscot always end too quickly, and the following day was no exception. After supper came more visiting and elbow bending, then more stumbling around in the dark before struggling again with my sleeping bag's zipper, then the welcome stillness of the Maine night. I hadn't been tired the previous night—oh, I *thought* I was, but tonight I *knew* what tired really was.

Dad sat upright at the first sounds of another nighttime raid outside our tent and poked his flashlight out the through the zippered tent flap.

"It's those damn raccoons again," he said.

I groaned. "Same bunch as last night, Dad?"

Evidently my father had had enough of the 'coon wars too, because he hesitated a moment, then snapped off his light. "It's hard to tell," he said. "They're all wearing masks."

I giggled myself to sleep.

The Fellow
in the Red Hat

THE SLEIGH BELLS on the door struck up a friendly clamor as the pair of men entered the store, accompanied by a cold blast of November wind. The first man waved an answer to the greetings from the others gathered around the stove as he emptied and hung up his canvas shooting coat. His name was Burt. "That coffee smells good already, Barney," he called to the storekeeper.

A small balding man looked up from filling a percolator, past Burt to where the second man still stood at the open door, peering out into the gathering darkness. "Gene!" the storekeeper called sharply. "I ain't heatin' the outdoors, for cryin' out loud."

After a moment an English setter entered the store, and Gene closed the door behind him. The dog went directly to the stove and accepted the greeting pats of the two men sitting there. Then, after walking several small circles, he lay down heavily on the worn wooden floor.

From his game pocket, Gene took three grouse and placed them next to those of his hunting partner on the wide ledge by the window, then he hung his shooting jacket over Burt's. He grinned as he addressed the storekeeper's permanent scowl: "Better that the dog keeps you waiting a mite, Barney, than to start doing his business here in the store." (If you've been to northern New England, you'll know the way Gene spoke that sentence: It sounded more like: "Betta thet the dog keeps you waitin' a mite, Ba'ny, then t' staat doin' his business hea' in the stoaa." All five of the men spoke with what other people referred to as a Yankee accent.)

Next to the stove Herb leaned forward until the front legs of his chair touched the floor. He examined the row of birds on the window ledge from over the tops of his spectacles. He shifted his chew before he spoke. "It appears that you fellows had quite a day of it."

Burt nodded. "We did take a few . . ." He pulled a chair close to the stove and sat between Herb and Doc Wood. "But that's not the half of it."

"The birds we took aren't much of a story compared to that strange fellow in the red hat that we ran into." Gene took a tin of Edgeworth from the tobacco shelf. A cash register sat on the counter, its perpetual "No Sale" sign and yawning cash drawer as much a part of the scene as the shaded hanging lamps and stacks of canned goods on the shelves. Gene tossed a pair of coins into the open drawer.

Without looking up, Barney said, "Pipe tobacco is seven cents, Gene. It has been since last spring." He closed the lid on the percolator and set it on the stove.

Gene tossed a second penny into the drawer. "Christmas! This is getting to be an expensive habit."

Without smiling, Barney casually mentioned, "I see milk prices are up again." Gene, a dairy farmer, grinned to himself as he filled his pipe. He sat on the edge of the woodbox, with his setter at his feet.

"What's this about a strange fellow?" Doc Wood spoke to Burt as he folded the newspaper he had been studying and slipped it between his leg and the arm of his chair. His flannel shirt seemed incongruous with his gray suit jacket and well-groomed appearance until one noticed he also wore briar pants and rubber-bottomed pacs.

"Yes, I guess he was strange . . ." From his shirt pocket Burt removed a flattened package of cigarettes and stared at it absently for a moment. "A nice enough fellow, but the whole day was a strange one." He slid his finger into the opening and tore through the top of the pack, offered a cigarette to Doc Wood, and took the last for himself. "Let me tell you about it—I want you fellows to understand that this is no bull . . ."

"*Pshaw!*" Herb spit into the label-less tin can he carried when he chewed indoors. "Here we go again: The only difference between a fairy tale and one of Burt's stories is that the one starts off with 'Once upon a time' and the other starts with 'this ain't no bull.'"

There was good humor in Herb's voice, and Burt chuckled with the others. After a moment Burt began, "Gene and I were supposed to make a day of it, but he had the vet up looking at the herd this morning, so Count and I poked around a bit in the alders below the farm."

At the sound of his name the setter near the stove looked up, then rested his head back on his forepaws. His shape and lines were classic, and even in repose he seemed graceful. Gene reached down and scratched the dog's ears as Burt continued.

"The first I saw of him was that red hat . . . Never saw red that bright before—like fire, almost." Burt leaned forward and lit his cigarette from the match that Doc offered. "I was just going into the woods—it must have been about ten—when that red hat caught my eye up the road, then him and his setter came out of the fog. The fellow walked right up to me like I should have been expecting him— stuck out his hand: 'Mister Spiller,' he says, 'I was afraid I'd missed you.' I didn't know him from Adam."

"A bird hunter?" Doc Wood asked.

"He appeared to be: He had that good-looking setter with him, and he had a nice little double under his arm." Burt winked broadly as he added, "I should have figured right then that the fellow had no sense at all: He was carring a twenty-bore."

Gene grinned. He was the only one of the four hunters who used a 20-gauge gun.

"I figured one of you fellows must have sent him down to find me, but he said no . . . Said that he'd traveled a long ways to hunt with me and Count. He had on his hunting clothes and looked normal enough . . . Except for that red hat."

"He knew both you and Gene's dog here by name?" Barney squinted one eye as he spoke.

"He did. Told me his name—darned if I can remember it—and said that he was a writer. I could tell by his accent that he wasn't from these parts. I still couldn't place him, but he wanted to hunt with me in particular—me and Count, here. The dogs seemed to tolerate each other, so I told the fellow I'd be pleased to have him along if that's what he wanted but that I'd be hunting with Gene after lunch. 'Sure, sure,' he says. 'I can only stay a few hours, anyway.'"

The squint on Barney's face intensified. "This is the same fellow who came a long ways to hunt with you? He can't stay more than an hour or two?"

"It didn't make sense to me, either." Burt shrugged. "We walked down to the brook crossing and started in. Nearly right off the dogs moved a bird from the hemlocks in there . . . An easy enough shot, left to right. When I took the bird, the fellow in the red hat says to me, 'I thought you only shot birds over points?'"

There were snorts of amusement from the listeners. "I hear tell of partridge shots that're that good." (Herb pronounced the word "paa-chige.") "Never can seem to meet up with them, though—seems they've either moved out of state or kicked the bucket a few years back."

Gene laughed. "Barney would have to quit stocking shells if all he sold depended on birds killed over points."

The storekeeper sat with arms folded, scowling. "I just might stop selling 'em anyways if you an' Burt don't stop wasting my time with these cock 'n bull stories of yours."

"Cock 'n bull!" Burt feigned incredulousness. "I know I might have told a few stories in my time . . ."

"*A few!* There's an understatement."

". . . but what makes this one so tough is that it's true." Burt paused a moment before continuing the narrative. "We worked that whole area down there, but the dogs couldn't seem to hold any of the birds . . . You know how skittish they can be in a quiet fog like we had this morning . . . And as soon as the dogs would get birdy, we'd hear the grouse roaring out fifty yards in front of us. The one bird that did come my way is still flying, for all the good my two shots did."

Herb nodded. "There's a lot of space around 'em."

"The fellow in the red hat was getting curt with his setter—he wanted to show her off a bit, but the birds weren't cooperating." Burt shook his head, remembering. "Why, I told him, you can't blame a dog for bumping a jumpy bird." Burt thought for a moment, then added, "This fellow had a few funny ideas—first there was that business of me only taking birds over points, then I had to tell him a dog only shows you where the grouse are . . . He doesn't hypnotize them, for goodness sake."

Doc Wood sat back in his chair, having arrived at a conclusion. "Probably a quail hunter. Remember when Barney's brother-in-law came up from Carolina to hunt with us? He thought the dog should point every bird too."

Burt considered this for a moment. "That brother-in-law was a feather merchant—no offense, Barney—but you could tell right off he was a phony. I don't believe he's much of a quail hunter back in Carolina, either." Across from Burt, Barney nodded his head in agreement. "But this fellow in the red hat this morning knew the game, all right. Just the way he moved through the woods and handled his dog made it plain he was a grouse hunter.

"We finished working out that brook bottom and came out onto Potter Road. The fellow checked his watch . . ." Burt brightened and clapped his leg. "He was wearing it strapped to his wrist like a bloody Englishman! Well, he said he only had an hour or so left before he had to go. I figured we'd hunt up behind the old Pratt place . . . That would put us back out onto Brickyard Road about the time I told Gene I'd meet him.

"Up until then, neither dog showed us much . . . Not that his lady setter was all that bad, you understand, but the birds were so skittish that even *Count* couldn't handle 'em." Heads nodded around the stove. The friends had all hunted behind the dog Burt would later call the one best he had ever known. "At the end of the old orchard up there, his dog hit as classic a point as you could ever hope to see. Count came up and backed, and it was prettier than that picture there . . ." Burt indicated the Arnott reproduction on the Peters Cartridge Company calendar behind the counter. "I waited for the fellow to go in and take the shot, seeing as how I already had a bird, but he waved me ahead. That grouse held until I got out in front of his setter—that's how well his dog had him pinned. It was an easy going-away shot, but the fellow carried on like I'd just won the war." Burt mimicked the man's clipped speech: "'Burton Spiller actually shot a grouse over my setter.'"

Herb spit a brown stream into his makeshift spittoon. "You mean there's somebody else who calls partridge 'grouse'?"

"I guess the fellow had some sense after all." Burt grinned. "Within a few minutes, Count found the bird's partner. Doc, if you thought this fellow might have been a four flusher, you should have seen him handle that shot. The bird flew right at him—you know how that can fluster the best of 'em—he just turned around and took the bird going away." Burt was on his feet, demonstrating how the stranger had ducked away from the close-passing grouse, then turned to take the shot. "His dog made a pretty retrieve from some thick juniper, too." He paused a moment. "Another strange thing about this fellow: He sat down and dressed out that bird just as soon as his setter brought it to him. That's it—the bird on the left, there." Burt pointed to a hen grouse on the window ledge. The bird had some oak leaves protruding from its open body cavity.

"Why didn't he keep the bird after going to all the trouble of dressing it out?" The beginnings of disbelief had crept into Herb's tone.

"He did . . . at first." Burt held up his hands. "But hold your horses, I'm coming to that part."

"Coffee's ready." Barney sniffed the steam coming from the pot, then went to the counter and passed out five well-used coffee mugs. Doc Wood held out his cup for a tentative sample.

"Well . . ." Barney looked expectantly at Doc. "How is it?"

"It could use a little . . . something." Doc held up a finger, mocking seriousness. "And I think I've got the something it needs." He produced a pint bottle from his jacket pocket.

"Ah-ha." Gene smiled. "I've always respected Doc's professional opinions."

Barney poured the coffee, and Doc added a shot of whiskey to each cup. He automatically skipped Burt's. "For medicinal purposes only, you understand." He grinned, and even Burt, a teetotaler, chuckled.

"Yes indeed," Barney lifted his cup toward Doc. "A little rye is the best thing that ever happened to a cup of coffee."

"Especially at this time of the day." Gene nodded. "Anything new on them making this stuff legal again, Barney?"

"Naw. Ratification has been out of the papers these past few weeks with the election coming up. Last I heard they were shy four states. It'll be next year, more than likely." Barney was the only one among them who regularly read the newspapers during hunting season.

"Go ahead with your story, Burt. I've got a feeling we're just coming to the good part." Herb came close to smiling. Barney strad-dled his chair seat with his arms crossed over the back. Doc tasted his spiked coffee, added a bit more whiskey to his cup, then offered the bottle to Herb. Only Gene sat away from the stove. From the woodbox he watched the listeners rather than Burt.

"I'm not so sure I won't have some of Doc's barley juice when all this is over." Burt ground out his cigarette under his boot, and there was a long pause before his rumbling voice continued. "We came out and sat on the wall while we waited for Gene. The fellow in the red hat said to me, 'I came a long, long way to hunt with you, Mister Spiller,' . . . He was still calling me mister . . . 'and spending some time with you has cleared up a few things I always suspected were true but wouldn't let myself believe.'" They all smiled at Burt's imitation of the stranger's accent. "'Why,' I told him, 'I've yet to see *any* bird dog that'll handle *half* the grouse he finds, let alone point every one in the woods. The nature of the bird is just too wary to let himself get pinned down consistently. They were that way when my father first took me hunting down Maine, and I expect they'll never change. Why, what makes grouse hunting such grand sport is that a dog *can't* point them every time.'"

"Amen," muttered Doc.

"'And don't believe the man who tells you he only takes his birds over points . . . at least, not if he's speaking of grouse. A dog on point is a lovely sight, but there's lots more to the sport than that,' I told him.

'That Foster fellow down in Massachusetts thought up that clay pigeon game to practice grouse shooting, and all those long crossers and overhead shots sure aren't chances you'd get over a dog on point. When it comes to grouse, every hunter I know takes 'em as they come.'" Burt shook his head and paused to sip his coffee.

"Where in hell did the man get ideas like that?" (Herb pronounced the word "idea" with an "r" at the end.)

Burt replied slowly, with the air of a man who is listening to his own thoughts. "When I asked him the same question, he said he had read my books . . ."

"*Pshaw!* You can't learn hell from breakfast about bird hunting from some *book!*" Herb sputtered.

"A tin horn," Doc pronounced disgustedly.

Burt was silent. His thoughts were on the collection of disconnected paragraphs in his desk drawer at home. He had never before so much as tried to write anything, but just this fall he had assembled some thoughts for an essay. He even had a title in mind: "His Majesty, the Grouse." That was the sum total of his writing "career." But, unlike his friends around the stove, he had understood the stranger's meaning clearly: The books the fellow in the red hat had spoken of were written by him, Burton Spiller. What could the man have possibly meant?

Doc's slow blink warned of the coming barb. "I don't believe this fellow in Burt's story was a hunter at all—he sounds more like a fiddle maker who got his strings a mite too tight."

The jibe was aimed at Burt, and he laughed along with the others. The ribbing never ceased. Barney hastened to counter, "Or maybe a doctor treating himself for a cold."

Doc raised his coffee mug. "Nothing wrong with that—of course, I'm about a dozen colds ahead of myself right now."

Gene got to his feet. "Hey, let me show you the shells he gave me to try." Gene crossed to where his shooting coat hung on the wall. Count's eyes followed him.

"I forgot all about them, Gene." Burt's voice held renewed enthusiasm. "What was it he called them—*plastic?*"

"That's it . . . Don't know why, though . . . They seem to be made of Bakelite or some varnished stuff." Gene searched through his coat pockets. "At first I thought they were some sort of fancy European shell, but they say Peters on 'em plain as day, even though they're colored yellow . . ." Gene trailed off, muttering to himself as he brought forth only the familiar blue paper cases from his jacket. He searched into his pants pockets. ". . . If I can just *find* the damn things."

"Maybe you used them," Burt suggested.

Gene shook his head. "Five shots—five empties." He picked out several spent hulls from the handful he held. "I don't see how I could have, but I must have lost the three of them."

Burt looked around at the expressions of amused disbelief that ringed the stove. "I *saw* that fellow give those yellow twenty-gauge shells to Gene, and I saw Gene put them into his coat pocket, there."

Gene came back and sat on the edge of the woodbox. "Burt was with that fellow in the red hat when I pulled up. The fellow knew my name too . . . called me 'Mister McCrillis' . . . Burt must have told him."

Burt shook his head solemnly. "No."

Gene continued, the narrator now. "Well, we chewed the fat for a few minutes, the three of us . . . I even asked the fellow who he was voting for tomorrow . . . Now listen to this—when I asked him, he said with a straight face, 'Who's running?' 'Why,' I told him, 'President Hoover and some Democrat name of Roosevelt. Where've you been? It's been near the only thing in the papers for months.' 'Well,' he said to me, 'I'd put my money on Roosevelt . . .'"

"*Pshaw!*" There were laughs of surprise from the three listeners. "First this fellow don't know so much as *who's* in the race, then he's going to bet cash money on a man who don't have a snowball's chance in hell!" Barney shook his head in unison with the others.

"*Roosevelt!* Come on, Gene." Doc Wood smiled.

"That's pretty much what I told the fellow—Hoover's a sure thing. But he said New Hampshire isn't the whole country." (Gene pronounced the state as three words.) "And when the votes were counted, Hoover would be looking for a job."

Barney's scowl nearly disappeared as he poured more coffee. "Why didn't you bring this fellow around to the store so we could have taken him up on that bet?"

"Hell, I'd have taken some of his money, too," Herb added.

Burt looked from face to face as Barney refilled his mug. "You'd best tell them about the tobacco pouch too, Gene."

Gene spoke from behind a cloud of smoke as he relit his pipe. "When I took out my pipe here, the fellow was quick to offer me some of his tobacco. But then he looked at that strapped-on watch on his arm—you'd think he'd seen a ghost. 'I've got to go,' he says, and without so much as a good-bye, he called to his dog and set off, nearly running down the road into the fog. 'I'll give you a lift,' I yelled after him, but I never heard him answer." Gene paused. "He wasn't gone more than a moment or two when I noticed his fancy tobacco pouch sitting on the fender of the Ford where he left it. Burt and I figured we'd just catch up with the fellow and give it back, so we cranked her up and headed after him . . ." Gene trailed off, thinking.

"Well . . ." Herb grew impatient.

"Maybe this is the strangest part of all—we hadn't gone more than a hundred yards when we found that partridge he shot, laying right in the middle of the road there. We drove at least a mile down Brickyard Road, but we never saw anything more of that fellow in the red hat . . . What's that matter, Burt?"

"I put that fellow's tobacco pouch in my back pocket, and it's gone now."

Gene started to get up. "I'll go look in the Ford. Maybe it slipped out."

Burt looked more baffled than ever. "How? I buttoned the flap." There was a silence.

"Probably in the same place with Gene's yellow shells." Barney shook his head, then with a wave of his hands got up in disgust and towed his chair back toward the counter.

"Pretty good, Burt, pretty good." Doc turned to Gene. "But you fellows must have had to rehearse your parts. That's a new touch."

Gene's frown said that he wasn't used to being doubted. "Listen— this *ain't* some tall tale, dammit."

"Of course it ain't." Herb took out his chew and deposited it into the tin can. "But, then again, it ain't nearly as good as that story Burt had last week about the cemetery up in the Desolation Covert. Maybe you ought to have the fellow using a gun that shoots lightning, or maybe a wolf instead of a bird dog . . ."

Doc grinned openly as he got up. "Like I said before, Burt: With yarns like that you ought to take up story telling full time."

Gene said nothing, but Burt noticed by the way he chewed his pipe stem that he was just barely holding his Irish temper. Burt reached across and patted Gene on the arm and said privately, "Easy, boy." He winked, and Gene returned a nod, tightlipped though his expression was.

In his inside pocket Doc discovered a list in his wife's handwriting and handed it over to Barney. While the storekeeper filled a box with groceries from the list, Doc began the latest traveling salesman story. Herb headed for the back room, unhitching his suspenders as he went. Gene sat in silence for a few minutes, then got up and went through the pockets of his shooting jacket once more. He shook his head no in answer to Burt's questioning look.

"I'll be stopping by the store in the morning," announced Doc, "and I'll be happy to give anyone who's here a lift to the polls." Then he smiled and added, "That is, providing there's no more talk of the Democrats winning."

Burt hadn't heard the pique. He sat deep in thought. The stove door clinked open as Barney added another chunk of split chestnut to the fire. Count rested his head against Gene's double where it leaned against the woodbox, and his master idly rubbed the dog's ears. Herb returned, and the conversation drifted to the coming winter, then to the Depression, then, inexorably, to politics. Burt remained quiet, but Gene saw his faint smile. When the moment was ripe, Burt drew out his billfold and removed all the folding money it contained.

"About that election tomorrow." Burt's tone was casual, and he let a five-dollar bill slip to the floor. "I've just got a hunch, you understand . . . I'll match anybody even money who'll see my bet on—what was that Democrat fellow's name again?"

Showers,
Heavy at Times

To find birds, you've got to go where they are. Not where they ought to be. Not where you'd like them to be. Not where they'd be easy to shoot.

—Havilah Babcock

"You're going out?"

I nod.

"In this rain?"

Another nod.

"You've already got two sets of clothes drying in the cellar from the past two days, and you're coughing . . ."

"Hon, we've already been over all this." I finish tying my boots and stand up to go.

"You've said yourself that you never have much luck in the rain . . ."

"No more, huh?"

As I start from the kitchen, Win gets up from her rug and goes to the door, waiting to be let out. My wife hands me my thermos. "I'm sorry, Steven. I just don't want you coming down with pneumonia."

"I know. I'll be back sometime this afternoon."

"Good luck. I love you."

"I love you too."

The weather follows the news, so I sit in the truck for an extra few minutes, parked on the drive into the Electric Fence Covert.

". . . *the Travelers weather outlook is for showers, heavy at times, continuing throughout the daylight hours with temperatures ranging into the high fifties . . .*" Pretty much a repeat of forecasts I've been hearing all week.

Win sniffs and squats a half-dozen times while I pull on rain chaps and uncase the gun. We walk down the dirt drive and cross the little bridge, then I cast her into the cover along the brook. One thing about the rain—no matter where we hunt, we have the place to ourselves.

The covert is wet. The brush, the grass, the trees, the air itself is saturated. It is impossible to remain dry on a day like this. No matter how you dress, it's just a matter of time. The alternative is to sit at home and hope the woodcock will halt their migration until the weather turns better. November rains being as they are, Win and I spend many outings getting wet while trying to stay dry.

Gunning in the rain does have its pluses . . . Not many, to be sure, but it's not all sweating yourself wet inside a rainshirt. There is beauty: Autumn's brilliance lies now on the ground, the last of the leaves having been driven down by the week's rains. Only the occasional white oak is not naked, though its leaves are reduced to pale shards. The indirect light of the overcast sky lends an even brightness to the covert, and unexpected colors emerge on the wetted surfaces of rock walls and tree bark. With the foliage screen gone, birds can now be seen on the wing for more than just the blink of an eye. And it's quiet. The ear-filling sound of dry autumn leaves underfoot is all but absent in the rain. The hushed swish of wet branches against my clothes is the only sound as I follow Win's bell through the brush.

We pass through a stand of high-branched white pines. I keep looking up into the dark canopy, hoping to see a grouse before he flushes, but it's a talent I don't have. I feel the bird's wing beats before I catch sight of him. I turn, watching the bird, and fire twice. He is wet, and the hollow noise of his wings can be heard for a few long seconds after I lower my gun. Overhead shots are not my forte. I practice them on the skeet range but regularly miss them in the coverts.

Win comes in and eyes me. I know she can't be aware of anything other than that I've fired at something, and now she's looking for instructions. Still, as always, I imagine an accusative look in her eyes. I put the empties in my pocket and close the gun on two fresh shells. A pair of smoke rings pops from the barrels.

The grouse headed up where the dirt road forms a barrier. He won't cross an opening if he can help it, so it's a good bet we'll find him on the near edge of the road cut.

We work the cover along the drive. The grouse has landed in another pine, and waits until I have passed beyond him before departing. He crosses the road and is gone before I can see him. Birds like that are best left for another day.

In the orchard Win points, but then tiptoes ahead when I approach her. I have grouse on my mind and react too quickly when a woodcock takes wing beyond the next apple tree. I put two more empties in my pocket, accept Win's comments, and put my shooting glasses back into their case. They are now beaded with water and are more hindrance than help. A miss like that one needs an excuse, and "obscured vision" is as good as any.

Within a hundred yards Win points again. She holds as I walk in front of her, but no bird gets up. I glance back at her, and she is looking off to her left. I move there. No bird. Now she is looking farther to her left, almost behind her. I move there, and two woodcock spring up—my annual chance at a double. I take the far bird cleanly, then pivot to try for the second bird back over my head. I fail to hold under him and miss.

Win brings in the bird, and I scratch her behind a wet ear. I ask if she scented the birds moving or merely spotted them sulking away from my approach, but she just smiles her open-mouthed dog's smile and won't tell.

We begin to cross a low marshy area, always wet but now spotted with standing water. I am in up to my ankles when I notice that Win, fifteen yards ahead of me, is doing the dog paddle. I retrace my steps and elect to take the long way around to the upper orchard. We must cross through the slash of a recently timbered area, and the going is rough. Win is on game the last two hundred yards while I attempt to hurry after her. We are still sixty yards out in the slash when a grouse, then two more, take wing into the evergreens beyond. I am encouraged that they are moving about in spite of the rain, although these three have seemingly vanished. After a couple of fruitless passes through the hemlocks we continue on our way.

The upper orchard holds two more woodcock for us, both pointed and taken nicely. Beyond the old farmhouse is "woodcock corner." If there are no other woodcock in the world, there will be at least one here. Win finds him. But the underbrush is thick where her bell stopped, and the bird gets up while I am still searching for the dog: I hear first the bird's twittering flight, then Win's bell again.

But he is not the last woodcock in the world, because Win points his partner within a hundred feet. The bird flushes immediately and swerves behind a small pine. I have the proper lead on him and fire. Every cluster of pine needles acts like a paintbrush in the rain, holding a droplet of water at its end. The result is an explosion of spray as the individual shot pellets pass through the bush, leaving me with no idea if the woodcock fell or flew on. Win searches behind the pine and brings in the bird to answer my question.

We walk back along the dirt drive. In places it is carpeted with fallen swamp maple leaves, all the more crimson for having been washed bright by the rain. Do I love this beautiful season because I hunt? Or do I love hunting as much as I do because it takes place here in autumn?

Reflected in a puddle is a single scarlet oak leaf, nearly luminescent in its brilliance. The leaf rests lightly on a discarded fence post that is frosted with emerald green moss. I dig out my little camera to capture the scene, but before I can click the shutter, a breath of breeze flips the leaf into its own watery reflection. I attempt to replace it but cannot recreate the delicate balance, and the resulting photos are of nothing more than an ordinary leaf on a soggy piece of wood. Autumn, and her beauty, are too quickly gone.

I REMOVE my rain shirt and chaps in an attempt to dry out while I drive. The rain has made inroads around the neck of my sweater, and though my feet are still dry, my pants are wet up to the knees. It won't be much longer before the dampness begins to work its way down the tops of my socks. The windows of the truck fog up, and the cab is filled with the not unpleasant odor of wet bird dog. Win rests her head on the transmission hump in the floor, snoozing. It's fifteen minutes to our next stop, the twin covers of Rodger's and Burned Barn.

TODAY Burned Barn holds only an owl, who eyes us suspiciously as we approach his roost high in an oak. He glides off, eerily silent, when we are still fifty yards away.

I emerge from the covert wetter by an hour and pause for some coffee from the thermos before crossing over into Rodger's. Win looks comically out of proportion with her normally fluffy coat soaked to peaks of meringue. She shivers a bit while waiting for me. There is water inside my rubber-bottomed pacs now. My thoughts run to the pair of dry boots in the truck. A fast pass through Rodger's and then I'll change. There are spare clothes in my war bag too. Thinking of them makes my sweater feel all the more wet under my rainshirt.

WE WORK UPHILL at Rodger's. Under a twisted old apple tree a windfall is still showing white where something has picked at it recently. I examine it: Lots of animals eat wild apples, but this one doesn't seem to have been gnawed by teeth. A grouse was eating here within the last few minutes. I look about, thinking of hiding cover. No place seems more obvious than the next, so we head farther uphill.

A deadfall. A stand of hemlocks. A tangle of thorns. I send Win to the unlikely side of each one while I walk the other. A stone wall. I send Win over, and as I turn, the grouse flushes fifty yards down the wall and is gone in a moment. I stare at the woods, hoping for a clue.

I get what I am looking for: nothing, really, just a flash of motion. It could be the movement of a distant tree limb, but it is enough to base a hunch on. I tell myself that what I saw was the grouse moving through the woods after making his turn. If that's true, then he has swerved to the right, heading for the birches beyond the fence. I whistle Win ahead, beginning a circle that will take us through the birches at a right angle to the bird's line of flight.

Ah, the power of positive thinking.

Win works the birch flats, dodging the prickly barberries and thorns that grow in clumps all around us. She is an all-day dog and can work at her easy trotting pace for as long as I care to walk behind her. Some men prefer a bigger ranging dog, but I've always thought more time is spent hunting for their dogs than for birds.

We pass out of the birches and cross the fence into the old pasture. Have I guessed wrong? More positive thinking: The grouse is here, but our cast through the birches missed him. We walk up the fence a bit and begin a second pass back the way we came. A hundred yards in the bird erupts from the far side of a thorn tangle, retreating toward my rear and the overgrown pasture. The shot is easy—fifteen yards, a natural pivot off my left shoulder. I see the grouse clearly: He is steel gray, and by the proportions of his tail, he is most definitely a "he." On shots like this I can never really recall my own actions but can accurately recount every move the bird makes. He passes close and shows me his belly for a moment as he banks away. I fire too fast, as I do with close birds, miss, and then cannot swing fast enough for a second shot. I watch the woods again but this time see nothing in the way of clues.

I look back at Win. "Hey, you get paid to point those things!"

In reply I get the open-mouthed smile again. The balloon caption over Win's head should read, "And you're supposed to shoot 'em—so what else is new?"

Chase him? Or hope he will still be there on the way out? He may calm down by then. On the other hand, he may be done feeding for the day and may fly out of the old pasture to roost in some pines. My chances of getting a good shot at him are slightly worse than my chances of finding him a third time—I've already used up a lot of luck on this bird, after all.

I squish my toes inside my boots. There are little puddles in there now. The grouse and the old pasture are between my wet feet and the truck. The deciding vote is cast, and we begin a loop that will take us back through the old pasture and then out.

Ten minutes later Win stops in midstride with a hind foot hanging in the air as she points to her left. Her high head indicates a long-distance point. I move forward. The grouse is here, but not where

Win's point says he is—he roars into flight from behind the next juniper tangle, screened by a cedar twenty yards out. I duck to the right to get clear, but he swerves left and stays hidden by the dense branches, and the time for a shot evaporates. A hundred yards out I see him top some cedars, then turn right, heading downhill.

I tip my wet hat. Three chances are enough for any gun. Admittedly there is a bit of the sour grapes attitude in my policy, but I will not chase any bird for more than three flushes.

I PULL into the driveway of the house I used to own. Fran Burland comes out onto the porch as I get out of the truck.

"Steven, you look like a drowned rat."

"Oh, you're just being nice. I'll bet you say that to all the fellows." I grin at her. "Can I borrow your garage to change my clothes?"

"Why don't you go into the cellar—it's lots warmer. I'll put on some tea."

Ten minutes later, slightly wrinkled but dry, I'm in the kitchen talking to my wife on the phone.

"Hi, Hon. I'm at a nice lady's house, and I just finished putting my clothes on . . ."

"You must be at Fran's. How's your tea?"

OVERLOOK ORCHARD is the next stop. It is the side of a mountain, really, where twenty or thirty years ago someone had a producing apple orchard. Indeed, there are still several piles of what were once apple baskets here, and where a long-handled picking basket was left leaning in a crotch, the tree has grown around the pole. Halfway down the hillside, in a flat open spot, a single chimney rises from the ruined foundation of a homestead. An old hardy rose still climbs on the foundation, having outlived the dreams of the one who planted it. The orchard is now overgrown into birches and popples, with alders near the bottom where a stream runs along the base of the hill. A hemlock forest climbs the opposite slope. There seems to be an abundance of grouse here year after year, and migrating woodcock stop among the apple trees. The covert is nearly perfect except for the fact that the hills seem to be getting steeper with each passing year.

My rain gear has dried out a little, and I have the renewed optimism that comes of dry clothes on a wet day. In the west a brightening sky promises clearing within the hour.

Win points my fifth woodcock before we are out of sight of the truck. The hillside is so steep that I approach her by moving from sapling to sapling, holding on with one hand to keep from slipping downhill. Win is rock solid and holds the bird in spite of my long and clumsy approach. I start to slide as I pass in front of her. The bird rises, twisting among the popple branches, but I'm still sliding. I sit down and poke the barrels in front of the bird, and he folds at my shot, falling from fifty feet above me to as many below. Win is determined, and after finding the woodcock, she fights her way back up the slope to make the retrieve to my hand. Small as it is, the limit bird weighs comfortably in my gamebag.

We pass behind the cellar hole. A flock of evening grosbeaks ignores the rain and our presence, intent on their feast of "doll's eye" viburnum berries from the bushes around us.

At the bottom of the hill we work the stream course for a couple hundred yards. At the end of the cover as I turn back uphill, Win suddenly strikes scent behind me at the edge of the brook. She surges ahead, then sniffs her way back along the bank. After shooting me a quick glance, she plunges into the rain-swollen stream and wades to the other side, then dashes across a small swampy area and points into a fallen hemlock tree.

There is no stepping stone to be seen, and haste is imperative. I am across in five quick steps. So much for my dry boots. The grouse will flush impossibly into the hemlocks beyond the deadfall, so one approach is as good as the next. I manage a dozen steps before he takes wing, flying not so much into the trees as under them in a curving, rising path. There is only one chance for a shot here, and I react quickly and thread the needle through the hemlock boughs— and connect!

Everything in the world is wet except for the grouse. His feathers float like cattail fluff and stick to everything they touch as if charged with static electricity. Win brings the bird to me, and we retreat to the edge of the brook to clean the grouse and remove the persistent fluff that now clings to both of us.

In the bird's empty body cavity I place a couple of small cold stones from the stream bed. Admiring the bird, I ponder the imponderable questions of bird hunting. Why is this bird dry? That his crop is full of ground greens indicates that he was moving around in the rain. He must have been feeding on the orchard side of the brook, then flown across to the fallen hemlock when he heard us coming. But how had Win known where he had gone? She went directly to the deadfall after she crossed the stream. Did she scent him from the other side? If she did, then how could she have walked within five feet of the grouse in the birches at Rodger's and not known he was there? And why had I been able to make this difficult shot, yet missed the gift opportunity at Rodger's? For that matter, why hadn't I seen that stone at the narrow spot in the brook where I could have crossed with dry feet?

I admire the bird's tail one last time, then slip him headfirst into my gamebag. Maybe if I always understood what the dog was doing and outguessed all the birds' maneuvers and connected on every shot, maybe then all the challenge would be gone from upland hunting. Maybe. One thing is for certain, though: A little consistency wouldn't hurt.

My truck is at the top of the opposite slope, which I noticed on the way down is indeed steeper than it was last year. Under the seat are my worn-out penny loafers with a ratty old pair of wool socks stuffed into them. The rain, which had stopped for awhile, now begins anew. Whatever signs of clearing I saw in the west have vanished. I open the gun and start back up the hill.

Rudie-ka-zudie

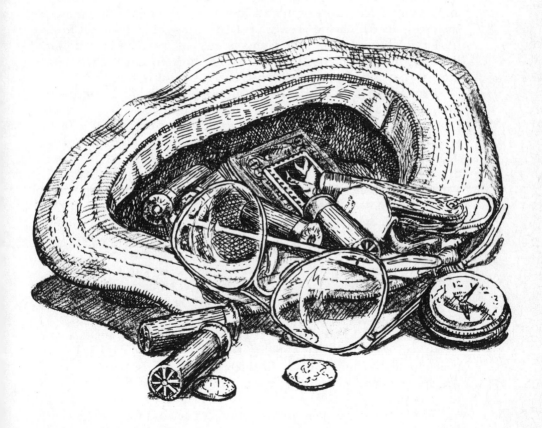

There are more things to admire in men than to despise.

—Albert Camus

IN THE FIRST moment that I saw the deer I thought he was a German shepherd: He was shaded in winter-gray and had his tail upturned, showing white as he moved along the far side of the wall. Hazel turned and looked at him as he approached, then barked nervously and retreated. He wasn't running so much as cantering easily through the open woods, having been spooked by something downhill from us. I didn't think to count the points on his antlers as he passed, but there were some in the front and some more in the back—eight, maybe ten points. Enough to impress even a non–deer hunter like me.

I don't see a lot of deer while I'm grouse hunting. Moving through the woods quietly is all but impossible, so I don't even try. Instead, I concentrate on being fast. And, of course, the dog wears a bell. Grouse don't seem to be overly alarmed by all the commotion, but deer hear me coming and stay out of the way. Once in a while I'll see one when I sit down to take a breather, but about the only time I surprise a deer is when I change directions abruptly. Or, as in this case, when something else spooks one.

I was hunting Hampden Basin. It shows on a topographical map as a bowl among the Wilbraham mountains in Hampden, thus the name. It's the sort of place where you hunt from one pocket to the next. There are remnants of abandoned apple orchards overgrown with barberries and cedar, some mature stands of hemlock between, and several little intense pieces of perfect grouse cover where a spring springs out of the mountainside. I would have named it "Grouse Heaven," except I had already called another covert by that name. Snow had fallen on Thanksgiving Day, and here on Friday I was trying to take advantage of the final few days of grouse season before the woods were closed for deer week, which lately had been stretched to ten days.

The buck's tracks were in the snow just beyond the wall. Mister Hancock once warned me to be careful of deer while I hunted his place: "This time of year they can be feisty—it's the *runting* season, you known." His warning was intended to be serious, but at the time his mispronunciation conjured up an image in my mind of a pugnacious buck calling a rival a "little runt." I've never been able to seriously consider the idea of deer as potentially violent creatures since.

I followed the line of tracks up the hillside with my eyes, hoping for another glimpse of the buck, but he had vanished into the netherworld where all game animals go once you blink. I wished him good luck in the coming week, although his being a ten-point buck in my corner of New England indicated that he had had more than his share.

Hazel and I had already determined that there were no grouse in the first orchard section, although we had followed a set of tracks for several hundred yards until they simply stopped. I had looked up quickly, hoping to find the grouse sitting in the tree immediately over my head, but that sort of thing happens more in outdoor stories than in life, and the only birds that occupied this apple tree were a pair of chickadees, busy doing whatever chickadees do in barren apple trees in the last days of November. I have sometimes seen grouse in trees before they flushed but seldom realized what I was seeing. I've also seen them running on the ground, usually just before they take off, but always assumed they were rabbits until it was too late to do anything but curse. On the other hand, I curse very effectively when required and am never at a loss for words.

The paths of everything that had passed through the woods during the previous twenty-four hours crisscrossed the surface of the snow: squirrels and mice and rabbits mostly, but there were several other sets of deer tracks, and in one of the spring coverts were the paw prints of a bobcat.

Against the far edge of the cover, where the woodland borders a farmer's pasture, I saw someone else's bootprints. I like to make believe that my coverts are secret places that only *I* know about, but there can be no deluding myself when there is snow on the ground. Unlike Robinson Crusoe, I wasn't thrilled to see another human footprint. It looked like whoever it was had passed within the past hour or so. I followed his tracks for a few hundred yards to see if I could determine what he was doing, and it soon became clear that the other printmaker was hunting—and probably for grouse. There aren't many people in the world with feet bigger than mine, but when I put my size 14 into his Vibram imprint, there was room to spare. There could only be one logical conclusion: Sasquatch had come out of the mountains and was hunting grouse in Hampden Basin. And had probably spooked a buck deer uphill a quarter-hour before.

Big Foot's path indicated he had hunted along the brook through the bottom of the valley—right where I had intended to go. I shook my head. There was a lot of cover on the high rim I hadn't hit on the way in, and rather than follow in another hunter's wake, I directed the dog back uphill.

Twenty minutes later Hazel produced a right quartering chance at a grouse in some cedar. The cover was thick, and although I heard the bird right away, when I finally caught sight of him, he was topping a little rise thirty yards out, and by the time I got the gun up, he was gone. Then from the other side of the ridge, I heard a single shot followed by a spoken curse, nearly as loud as the gunshot. A grouse hunter, and from his choice of curses, an experienced grouse hunter at that. I shouted hello, opened my gun, and went out to meet Sasquatch.

The man who had made the footprints was dressed in briar-proofs and a shooting jacket, size extra-extra large, maybe three extras.

"Sorry—I didn't mean to crowd you," he said. "I heard your dog's bell just before that partridge came out. I had a shot at him, but I blew it."

I knew this giant. His raspy high-pitched voice gave him away even though he wore a disguise that consisted of a mustache, grayed hair, and twenty-odd years of aging. "No problem." I smiled. "Did you ever hear of a Rudie-ka-zudie play?"

IN THE AUTUMN of 1962 my high school football team was a powerhouse that was favored to win the double-A conference: The offensive line was all seniors, and the defense was the same one that had only given up a handful of points the previous year. I was just a sophomore sub, but the regular center had sprained a shoulder in practice and I was about to play my first varsity game, against Greenfield.

The most outstanding talent on a team full of talented seniors belonged to the right guard. Yet, unlike so many others, he was not distracted by his own abilities. He went on to play for Michigan and, briefly, the Los Angeles Rams. He was a nice guy, and in spite of the pervading attitude among the upperclassmen on the team, he was a nice guy toward *everyone* on the team—even the subs. His name was Rudy Krizmardzick.

Against Greenfield, we were quickly second-and-one on the opening set of downs, and a short-yardage fullback dive play was called for. Greenfield lined up in an unexpected 4–3 defense, with down linemen in the gaps to either side of the center. Understand that on our team the center was responsible for last-second changes in blocking assignments, so even though this was only my second play from scrimmage, the time had come to act like a varsity center: I told the line, in code, that the right guard would double-team with me and that the left guard would block his man alone. What I said was "Rudie-ka-zudie and me."

Everything went right, and we opened a huge hole through which the fullback galloped for far more than the short yardage we needed. We broke the huddle and lined up again. Across the line the Greenfield captain, who had been on the receiving end of the double-team block and now looked like Beetle Bailey after being mauled by Sarge, motioned to a linebacker to cover the middle with him. "It looks like another Rudie-ka-zudie play," he said, which caused Rudy Krizmardzick to giggle out loud. There was always something infectious in his high-pitched laugh, and soon the whole line was laughing too. We were penalized five yards for delay of game, then another five when we still couldn't answer the "setdown" call. It was Rudy who couldn't stop, and his wonderful giggle couldn't be denied. On the sidelines the coach was screaming at us. "What's so damn funny out there?!"

It loses something in retelling. Like most good ones, you had to be there.

HE LOOKED HARD at me, but after twenty years we're all incognito to a degree. When I told him who I was, suddenly his face cracked into the grin that I recall from long ago. If I still hadn't recognized him, that would have given him away: Rudy's grin was and still is the quintessence of the wide-open smile of Polish people everywhere.

"Sure, I remember you," he said. "I heard someone quote you last year sometime—something about dog training—and I thought to myself, 'Hey, I know that guy.' I couldn't put the face together with the name, but now it all comes back."

It didn't seem that he was disappointed with whose face the name belonged to, and I took that as a small compliment. He had an ex-jock's job as a vice president of a sporting goods firm in another state but was in the area for his twentieth year high school reunion. He happened to be hunting in my grouse covert this morning after Thanksgiving because it was just up the road from his former in-laws' house, where he was staying while he was in town.

"Ever write about playing ball?"

"Not so far," I said. "Those were some tough times. Not many of my football memories are the kind I'd like to write about."

"Boy, isn't that the truth," he said. "What a bunch of assholes we had on that team. I don't even like to think about the kind of person I was back then."

I hadn't perceived him as qualifying to be included in that description, and said as much.

"Naw." He shook his head. "We were all a bunch of young studs, or at least tried to act that way. Thank God people change."

At length I realized who I was to him, and why he was excusing himself to me. There's a bunch of my own underclassmen to whom I'd like to say "I'm sorry" as well. Eventually we all escape the "runting" season, but the person we once were haunts us all.

So FOR AN HOUR or so we hunted together. Hazel showed off her pointing ability when we relocated the grouse, but there was no chance for a shot. It would have been nice if it could have been otherwise—maybe we could have double-teamed the bird for one last Rudie-ka-zudie play, but, like grouse sitting in trees at the end of a string of tracks in the snow, that sort of thing happens far more often in stories than in reality.

The morning warmed, and fog began to rise off the melting snow. I had earlier in the season taken a pair of birds out of Hampden Basin. They don't make any more grouse once the season starts—waterfowl and woodcock migrate through and seemingly replace themselves, and pheasants are released all during the fall, but the supply of grouse only diminishes as the season wanes. We hunted back along the curve of the hills, recrossing our own tracks occasionally, hoping a bird might have moved in since we'd passed earlier. None had.

We shared a cup of coffee at my truck, and I gave him a lift to the house where he was staying. We shook hands when we parted, and I was left wondering how well he really remembered me, if at all. What was there to remember other than a single incident in a half-forgotten football game? We weren't friends, after all, and who remembers underclassmen anyway? That was two years ago. I haven't seen him again, and in truth, I don't ever expect to again. Too bad, I thought. The random crossing of paths is just that—a most random of events.

But as I drove away from Hampden Basin that morning, I reflected that some things in life change, and others remain the same—even those you lose track of. A fellow I remembered as a nice guy had gotten twenty years older. He had survived his youth and, like the rest of us, had his share of regrets. "Thank God people change," Rudie-ka-zudie had said. But it is lucky, too, that some people never do.

Knuckleball!

It's not so much missing the little buggers that irks me so much as the looking so damn foolish doing it.

—Henry Mulak

I SLOWED as I drove around the last curve. Up ahead, where I had intended to pull off the road, another car was parked on the shoulder outside the Bondsville Covert. All during October I continually delude myself with the idea that cars parked by my woodcock coverts belong to hikers or mushroom pickers . . . anyone but another bird hunter. But there were no delusions possible this time: Two fellows in fluorescent vests were uncasing their shotguns. Maybe they were rabbit hunters. I crossed my fingers and stopped the truck abreast of them.

"How's it going, fellas?" They were among the ever-growing number of sportsmen who are considerably younger than I. One of them leaned in the truck window. He had a pheasant feather in his hatband.

"We limited-out on roosters this morning, so we thought we'd try our luck on partridge. We really don't know much about 'em—does this look like a good spot to you?"

I hoped he hadn't seen me wince. Although these two hardly seemed serious woodcock hunters, sharing my pet coverts with strangers is not my idea of loving my fellow man. "It looks to be as good as any," I said. "You're liable to find birds 'most anywhere this time of year."

There. I hadn't lied to them . . . I hadn't even *mentioned* woodcock. Smiling, I drove on, thinking I was foolish to worry—they wouldn't find much in there without a dog. I glanced in the rearview mirror just in time to see them let a Brittany out of their car's trunk. If I were a cowboy, what I muttered would be classified as a "discouraging word."

A half-mile farther down the road I stopped at another of my coverts. Around the cut-over areas the sassafras bushes were in lovely color, and my setter did some nice work on the two woodcock we found there. It wasn't until I was sitting on the tailgate with a cup of coffee that I took notice of the frequent shots in the distance. They sounded out in bunches of three and four rather than as single reports.

Driving back out to the highway, I passed the Bondsville Covert just as the same two fellows were coming out. Of the three, only their Brittany looked happy. I slowed to a stop. "Well, how'd you do?"

Their expressions said they wished I hadn't asked. "We found a *shitload* of birds in there."

"Great!" I tried to look sincere. "Where were they?"

"Everywhere." He shook his head. "Every time we turned around, the dog was on point. We finally ran out of ammo."

"No kidding. How many did you take?" The answer was so obvious that I wondered if the question wasn't a bit sadistic.

"Well . . . They were woodcock, you know." That served as sufficient excuse.

Later it dawned on me that I had seen ballplayers wear the very same embarrassed look: It was when they returned to the dugout after being struck out by a soft-throwing junk pitcher. As a matter of fact, I'd bet a nickel that the first pitcher to throw a knuckleball was probably a woodcock hunter.

WOODCOCK SEEM easy. They hold so well for even a mediocre pointing dog that there is seldom an element of surprise in their flush, and in a race with all the other gamebirds the woodcock is so slow that he'd finish dead last. Ah, but he's tricky. So much so that even if someone were able to point out his flight path ahead of time, it would be of little help to the gunner. I sailed with a chief engineer from the state of Maine who was a hunter. He contended that woodcock had more space around them than other birds. He may be right. They flutter up, plainly seen but too close for a shot, weaving their way through the overhead branches until they've found flight room, then they'll mindlessly dip back down into the trees again. Their unpredictable maneuvers and flank turns keep the gunner waving his gun like an orchestra conductor's baton. Then, after having been "woodcocked" several times in a row, the hunter finally steadies himself to wait out the bird's off-speed tactics. That's when the next one will blast off the ground like a grouse, buzzing away low and fast. As I said, they're tricky.

The habits of the timberdoodle so overlap those of the ruffed grouse that they're frequently found side by side in the same coverts. One bird is the ideal complement for the other: The quickness of a grouse's flush and the erratic dodges of a woodcock's flight are a combination that can keep anyone off balance. Frank Woolner made an accurate comparison when he stated that if the grouse is a high-performance jet fighter, then the woodcock is one of those bi-wing stunt jobs. The difference is never more evident that when a tense grouse hunter walks in over his dog's point, fully expecting the thunder of wings and instead flushes a woodcock. A bookmaker, if he's at all merciful, would refuse the bet: The tightly wound gunner will shoot too quickly and miss every time.

During the course of a morning in the uplands, woodcock will provide the hunter opportunities to use both the deliberate shooting style of the waterfowler as well as the snap-shooting methods of the brush gunner. Sprinkle a few grouse around the same coverts and you can begin to understand how so many spent shells can still add up to an empty gamebag.

LOOKING FOR and actually locating woodcock hunting areas are not necessarily the same exercise. If pinned down, the experienced woodcocker might say that the surest thing to look for when searching out a place to hunt woodcock is . . . woodcock. He would not be avoiding the question. The bird can be as unpredictable in his habits as he is in flight, and the birds are indeed where you find them. At times they'll concentrate in one small section of a covert, ignoring the rest of what seems an ideal area. They will sometimes continue to come to a favorite place long after it has been turned into a housing development, yet they will unexplainably stop visiting another spot that seems unchanged. Why . . .? Who knows.

An eerie feeling of déjà vu sets in when I revisit a covert and take a woodcock from *exactly* the same spot where I took one the last time. Sometimes it goes on all season long, and there's no escaping the feeling that maybe I only *thought* I shot the woodcock that was here last time, because *here he is back again!* Evidently birds from consecutive flights single out that one particular corner or tree as an ideal resting place, although what sets it apart from its surroundings is unobvious to me. Maybe there's a hidden aspect only woodcock see from the air—I've tried interrogating those that I've captured, but they never tell.

Occasionally when a once-flushed bird is pursued and flushed a second time, two woodcock will take flight. It happens too frequently to be shrugged off as coincidence: The first bird flew to join his partner. But how did he communicate and know just where to go? More mysteries.

There is a mistaken belief that woodcock depend entirely upon protective coloration for their survival. That idea is fine as it applies to hawks and dogless hunters, but what about weasels and foxes and

other scenting predators who hunt with their noses? The bird's camouflage doesn't keep my bird dogs from finding him, and I can't
imagine it hampers a hunting fox too much, either. It's a safe bet that
at night, when most of the fellows with the big teeth are on the prowl,
the woodcock is alert to danger and quick to take wing. It's only in
the daylight that he lets his guard down and relies on his protective
coloration.

Which leads to the idea that when a hunter's bird dog points a
woodcock, the bird may be sleeping off a long night of snagging
worms and dodging foxes. I know *I'm* not immediately "with it" when
I first wake up, and the fact that a woodcock may be both awakened
and flushed by the hunter's approach goes a long way toward explain-
ing some of the crazy things he does in flight.

There is an old joke that a woodcock's eyes are positioned so that
he can find holes in a shot pattern, and his stubby wings enable him
to fly right through them. Occasionally a 'doodle will get through a
pattern with only a ruffled feather or two, but that's simply because
there's a very small bird under those brown feathers. All gamebirds,
of course, are considerably smaller than their silhouettes, but it is
difficult to conceive of how tiny a target he really is until you hold up a
naked woodcock by the foot. (I'll guarantee you'll trade in your 7½s
for 9s after you do.) Those "hole-finding" eyes seem the strangest
thing about this strange bird until he is seen drilling for worms. Then
the utilitarian design of big, night-vision eyes that can see "up" while
his bill probes "down" becomes apparent.

As if to prove that they are not exclusively nocturnal birds, occasionally a woodcock will be taken with fresh mud on his bill or a live
worm in his mouth. A dog that strikes the meandering trail of one of
these daylight-feeding birds might appear to be working that debat-
able entity, *the running woodcock*. On occasion I have seen them, out of
impatience, walk out from a point. But any contention that woodcock
run is a sad reflection on the contender: In the world of gamebirds,
nothing holds better than a woodcock.

IT IS ONE of the happy coincidences in the sporting world that the
game of woodcocking, where a dog is an absolute necessity, also
happens to be the one sport where a dog needn't be a champion to do
a workmanlike job. The woodcock dog needs only to handle and to
have a modicum of manners. The birds are strongly scented and hold
so well for a point that the finer things expected in a grouse or a quail
dog are luxury options on the basic utility woodcocking model.

But the same reluctance to flush that makes the bird hold so well for even a sloppy point works against the dogless hunter. By chance, he'll almost step on one occasionally and get a shot. But for every 'doodle the hunter kicks up blindly there will be ten more squatting invisibly on the leaf mulch that he will walk by unknowingly. A dog— any dog—will *triple* the number of birds he finds, and a *good* dog will triple *that* number.

Although they hunt them joyfully and point them intensely, most bird dogs don't like to retrieve woodcock. Popular theories are that the bird is loose-feathered or bad tasting . . . Believe whatever explanation you like. Dogs do so many other weird things that cannot be explained logically that it's anybody's guess why they'll enthusiastically fetch in a nasty, clawing bundle that is a wing-hit pheasant but not a woodcock.

MOST TYPES of hunting, and fishing too, suffer a gap between the sport as it should be and the sport as it actually is. The sportsman's imagination can close the gap considerably if he can get out of sight of houses and parked cars. He can believe for a little while that he is hunting pheasants in the Nebraska farmlands rather than stocked birds on a state management area. Or that he is casting for steelhead on the Yellowstone rather than some local brook. But today's wood-cock hunting is just what it should be: The little patches of cover just outside of town are what sportsmen the world over conjure up when they dream of a woodcock hunting trip, and the suburban hunter can make of the game whatever he cares to and not have to pretend anything. A man doesn't have to go to New Brunswick or Cape May for the world's best woodcock hunting—it's probably right there at the end of his street.

If you pursue woodcock, you will meet others afield who are sure you're wasting your time. Some will sneer so boldly as to say they wouldn't waste a shell on a woodcock. (Obviously these men are chicken hunters. Why else waste a shell?) If a gaudy trophy of a bird strutting by the roadside can bring out the unsportsmanlike worst in some hunters, then woodcock, which are hardly trophies and rank considerably below chickens as table fare, can bring out the very best. Woodcock hunting, after all, is pure fun. Success in the October woodlands is measured in terms of the enjoyment the hunter derives from a day afield with his dog rather than the weight of his gamebag. And, in this case, the secret to this particular success lies in the fine art of not taking yourself seriously.

It seems a perverse human trait that at times we are able to derive enjoyment from our own failings. Woodcocking will do that to a man.

There is a hunter inside all of us, a hunter who takes pride in our shooting and knows that 'doodles are so easy we should never miss one. Each time we are "woodcocked" into poking a couple of holes in the sky, the hunter part of us is disgusted. Ah, but the other part of us, the human that offsets the hunter inside—he throws his head back and *laughs!*

WHEN THE SUMACS turn crimson and the calendar announces the autumn equinox, the woodcock hunter feels the press of the approaching season. The aspens follow the swamp maples into flame, and for a brief instant in time heaven becomes an overgrown pasture in New England, complete with stone fences and clear brooklets and feathers floating among the birches. The whole year was spent waiting for these few weeks, and they are seized with an urgency. Then one rainy day the autumn colors lie on the ground and the trees are bare again. And soon after the woodcock are gone. By mid-November the woodcock hunter has turned his full attention to grouse. The coverts are not the same . . . not worse, really, because grouse hunting is an addiction only postponed until after the woodcock migration. The woodlands are simply different. Like everything else worthwhile, the woodcock season is a fleeting thing. Impermanence, it seems, is a prerequisite to love—no one loves plastic flowers, after all. But if I were ever to find myself in a story where I was granted a magic wish, I'd be sure to inquire by how much I could lengthen the month of October before I made my decision.

Meat Dog

SANDY FOUGHT the wheel as the old Chevy bounced along the gravel road, bottoming out on nearly every bump. In the back seat both bird dogs complained in low mutterings, not quite barking out loud. The car hit a particularly large pothole, and on the passenger side John's head hit the roof. "*Christmas! Slow down,* for cryin' out loud."

"Sorry." Sandy shrugged. "I'm just about moving."

"You're doing fifteen on a ten-mile-an-hour road." John pointed at the floorboard. "The one in the middle—that's the brake. See it down there?" Sarcasm had been an integral part of their friendship since high school. After a moment John asked, "Is the Greek still behind us?"

Sandy reached back to move his Brittany's head out of the way, then glanced in the mirror and gave an affirmative nod. George's Chrysler, with its massive hood and fenders, pitched and yawed like some ocean vessel as it labored over the rutted road behind them. The spray of water that erupted each time one of the wheels hit a pothole only added to the illusion. Through the Chrysler's visored windshield he could see Jimmy sitting on the passenger side, holding on with both hands. Most likely he was pointing out the brake pedal to George too.

After a moment, Sandy said, "I don't think George and Jimmy are too crazy about this field trial idea, either." He referred to an earlier conversation.

"Shoot-to-kill trials are different—it'll be a good time."

"Well . . . You know me and field trials."

John considered his reply for a moment before he spoke. "With you, I don't think your problem is so much with field trials as field *trialers*."

Sandy smiled but said nothing.

When they reached the clubhouse, Sandy parked next to several other cars in the lot. John let the dogs out but held their collars. Both men wore rubber-bottomed pacs with their pantlegs tucked into the tops. George pulled up next to them.

The Chrysler's door swung open. "What a miserable road. I just had the wife wash the car, too." He opened the truck, letting two dogs out. George the Greek, as they called him, insisted in the face of criticism that the trunk of a car was the right place to transport a bird dog.

Sandy tapped at the window of the passenger side where Jimmy sat immobile. "Are you going to get out?"

The gray-haired senior member of the group rolled the window down, affecting disbelief. "The Greek's crazier than you are—he was going to pass you back there—on *that* road!"

George patted the woodwork on the '47 Town & Country. "This baby would have done it, too—except I changed my mind at the last minute when I saw you go out of sight in that pothole."

Their four dogs, once released, raced past the clubhouse and ran to the pheasant pens beyond. Two dozen roosters flew up at their approach, only to hit the overhead netting and fall back to the ground. The two setters and the springer ran back and forth excitedly, unsure of what they were expected to do with the penned birds, but Sandy's Brittany stood back, trembling as she watched more birds than she had ever imagined existed.

The dogs were whistled in. His companions headed for the clubhouse, but Sandy walked with his Brittany beyond the pens, as much to see the grounds as to stretch his legs after the hour's drive. Despite the melt going on, patches of snow still clung to the north sides of the hills and in the shadows of the rock walls that crisscrossed the fields and woods. Winter-as-usual in Connecticut was a tenuous season at best: cold one week and thawing the next. The potholes in the roads gave testimony to that fact.

His Brittany had a lenthy pedigree and a formal name, both in French, but his children had called the puppy Annie, and the name had stuck. As Sandy climbed the hill back to the clubhouse, an older man in a red plaid jacket crossed toward the pheasant pens. "What kind of a dog is that?" he called.

"A Brittany. I brought her back from Europe with me in 'forty-five."

"Make sure you get braced with a springer, then."

"Oh, she points just fine." By now, Sandy was used to conversations like this.

"A pointin' spaniel, eh?" The man squatted to rub the Brit's ears.

Sandy noticed he held his cigarette away from the dog. "She must be quite a meat dog."

"She's been called worse—sometimes by me."

The man smiled, then stood and offered his hand. "Tom Lamica. I'll be judging today."

Sandy introduced himself and shook the man's hand. "This is quite a set-up you've got here—and that's certainly a nice touch." He indicated the pheasant pens.

The older man laughed humorlessly. "Yeah, it was a good idea during the summer, but people don't turn out for a shoot-to-kill once hunting season's over."

"Your club should get some business today: I came with three other guys, and I hear Brownie and his bunch are bringing their dogs up today."

Tom squinted through his cigarette smoke, examining Sandy closely. "Are you part of that Windsor crowd?" From the way he spoke the term it was evident that Tom didn't have much use for anyone who was.

Sandy searched for an answer. No matter that "the Windsor crowd" looked down their noses at Sandy and his non–field trialing friends, geographical association said that he was guilty as accused. "Naw," he answered. "We don't have much to do with those chowder-heads. We're the Fox Pass Sportsmen's Association."

"Well," Tom smiled, and clapped Sandy on the shoulder. "Glad to have you boys with us today."

THEY WERE SITTING with their dogs in the morning sunshine on the clubhouse porch when Brownie's car pulled into the parking lot. It was a new '51 Ford convertible that had somehow survived the trip down the muddy road with its white wall tires and shine intact. Walt Christian's car pulled up next to the Chevy, and next to that, Bobby Bowman's truck with dog boxes on the back.

"Nice car," Jimmy observed.

Sandy looked from his old stove-bolt six to the new Ford, dazzling with chrome. He grinned. "I prefer running boards, myself."

"I think you left yours in that pothole back there," Jimmie replied seriously.

With little more than an exchange of nods, Brownie and his two friends walked past and into the clubhouse to sign up. As with actors, their dignity seemed controlled by a vague idea of their own importance. The door closed behind them.

"When people ask me about Mister Homer Brown," John said, "I tell them we have a nodding acquaintance—I say hello, and he says nodding. Me, I've stopped saying hello, but I notice he still says nodding."

Minutes later, Tom Lamica opened the door of the clubhouse. "Okay—it's ten o'clock. We've got seventeen entries. If you Fox Pass fellows want to come inside, we'll have the draw."

They looked at each other for a long moment. "Fox pass?"

"I think that's what he called us—'You fox pass fellows.'"

Sandy held up his hand. "For today, we're the Fox Pass Sportsmen's Association."

They turned on Sandy. "Are you serious?"

"It was either that or be part of 'that Windsor crowd.'"

There was a silence, then Jimmy nodded. "Fine. I'll even be the president."

They started into the clubhouse. "How do you spell that—Fox Pass or faux pas?" George had a way of laughing as he spoke.

John added, "I'm not sure I even want to be a part of any association that would have a low life like *me* as a member."

INSIDE, file cards with the names of the entrants and their dogs were placed in an empty number-ten can, then drawn two at a time in the order they would run. The two men with springers were purposely paired in the same heat, but the rest of the draw was random. When eight pairs of cards were thumb-tacked to the wall, there was one card left in the can. Tom took it out and double-checked to make sure it was the last one before reading the name that would run the final heat alone. The name on the card was Sandy's.

JIMMY RAN his springer, Max, in the first brace, and although Max performed in his normal workmanlike manner, the dog he was paired with ran out of control and, after wildly flushing both of the planted pheasants, chased one of them back to the pens. The rooster landed on the roof netting, and the other springer stood barking up at the bird. Jimmy just smiled and heeled Max in, but there was little humor in his eyes when he rejoined his friends on the clubhouse steps.

JOHN HAD DRAWN the third heat against one of Brownie's dogs. Sandy went with him to the breakaway, then stood talking with Tom and the other judge while they waited for Brownie to bring his dog to the line.

"So you do this once a month. I can see where it can be fun: hunting, with a little competition thrown in."

"Competition does funny things to people." Tom lit a Lucky as he spoke. "Hunting isn't enough for 'em. To have a good time, they've got to outdo somebody at something, so they take up skeet shooting or field trialing. This. . .," he motioned to the course they were about to run, ". . . is supposed to be just for fun, but there's some that get mighty serious about it." He lowered his voice. "Watch out for this Windsor crowd. They'll beat you to the bird field and shoot both birds if you give 'em half a chance."

"I've run with this guy before," John motioned to Brownie, who was just approaching. "I won't let him get in front of me."

THE BACK COURSE was fairly short, and within ten minutes of breaking away John's all-white setter appeared in the bird field, with Brownie's not far behind. By the time the judges and handlers appeared, both dogs were on separate points. Brownie hurried to his dog but missed an easy shot on the pheasant. The bird sailed over the trees beyond the bird field and, in answer to the hopes of everyone who had yet to run, headed for the back course. Brownie directed his setter to where John's stood on point, hoping to get credit for a back, but John knew the game, too, and flushed his bird quickly. The shot was an easy one, and John's setter was credited with a retrieve.

IN THE BACK SEAT of George's Chrysler Sandy opened his thermos and poured coffee into four paper cups. "I'd say they've got you in first, John."

"Aw, it really doesn't matter much to me. I got a nice point and saw a pretty retrieve, and for a moment I thought it was October again." He turned to Jimmy. "You and Max got a raw deal."

Jimmy waved his hand in dismissal. "You pay your two bucks and take your chances. That's the luck of the draw."

"Yeah, but it's not right." John shook his head as he handed a paper cup into the front seat. "Everybody's here to have a good time, but that guy had no business entering a dog that isn't interested in hunting."

"Well, Max hunts for my pleasure, not to impress some judge." Jimmy sipped his coffee, then added, "But still, I'd have liked a chance to make *my own* screw-up."

George laughed. "You got plenty of practice last fall." The two hunted together each weekend during the hunting season. "Where is Max, by the way?"

"He's in the trunk."

Sandy grimaced. "You're as bad as George. You could have put him in my car."

Jimmy looked out the side window at Sandy's dilapidated '37 Chevy. "I offered Max that choice," he said earnestly. "But he said he'd rather the trunk."

From the car they watched as the fourth brace arrived in the bird field: Out beyond the tree line, Walt Christian's big pointer topped a rise and streaked through the bird field and out the other side without slowing down at all. He ran past the pheasant pens and circled behind the clubhouse and parking lot and was just coming back into sight when the judges and handlers came into view. Walt was making obscure hand signals in the air, hoping to fool the judges into thinking his dog was doing just as he wanted him to. The pointer found a bird but never stopped, and although there was a moment when it appeared that the dog was going to fly into the air and catch the pheasant, at the last instant the pointer rediscovered gravity and the bird sailed over the trees.

"You're still in first, John." Sandy had rolled down the back window and was peering out at the action. "But wait a minute . . ."

The other man's dog had pointed, then began to creep forward. The rooster could be seen walking away in the short grass. The man quickly raised his gun and strafed the pheasant, then raced his dog to the bird.

". . . No, you're safe," Sandy said.

"That guy must go through a lot of dogs." George imitated the man's shooting form. "'Move your tail, Sparky—ka-blam!'"

"Yeah, he's mean all right." Sandy observed. "He probably keeps that dog in the trunk."

THE DAY wore on, with pheasants being planted in the field in front of the clubhouse for each successive brace of dogs. And as Tom Lamica had predicted, several men who had been unlucky enough to find themselves paired with one of "the Windsor crowd" found that when they reached the bird field both of the birds had already been efficiently removed. There could be no argument that the field trialers had good dogs: With the exception of Walt Christian's flying pointer, all of their dogs had at least one find, and Bob Bowman's classy setter had pointed three pheasants. It was the fierce competitiveness of Brownie and his friends that seemed so out of place among the casual hunters who had come to enjoy a warm winter's afternoon.

GEORGE'S TURN came up. After the judges had entered George's name and the name of his setter, he asked, "Any wild birds here?"

"There's always a few that escape from the pens. The place is pretty well hunted out during the fall, though." Tom turned to the other judge, "Sonny saw a rooster down by the swamp, when, Sonny? Last week?"

"Yeah, he was a *big* sommabitch." Sonny held his arm out to indicate that the pheasant was five feet long.

If one expects to win a field trial, one should refrain from laughing at the judges. George did not expect to win. "Jimmy," he said, "do you have an extra deer slug? Just in case we run into this bird?"

Everyone laughed, but Sonny just looked away.

George's Llewellin was paired with a dog that appeared to be his twin. The other setter's name was Freckles, and it seemed his owner had a running argument with him as they walked the back course: *"Freckles! What're you doin'? Get over here! Now get out front! What'd I tell you?! Freckles!"*

George said later, "If I had a dog that was smart enough to understand all that, I wouldn't even have to take him hunting. I'd just leave a note by his dog house and tell him what I wanted."

Freckles pointed a planted pheasant, but when his owner missed he took out his frustrations on the setter: he was put on a short lead and hauled off before the judge signaled "Pick-up."

"That poor dog." Jimmy shook his head. "I wonder what he did to deserve an owner like that."

"Maybe he was a Nazi in his last incarnation," John offered.

THE LAST BRACE finished at 2:30, and after taking a five-minute breather on the porch steps, the judges got to their feet. Tom waved to Sandy. "Okay, let's have a look at that pointin' spaniel."

His friends gathered around Sandy as he started for the breakaway. Jimmy put his hand on Sandy's shoulder. "Now listen, you've got to find more than just one bird. They must have that twerp Bowman in first with his three finds."

"Yeah, it's down to you, Sandy." John had his other shoulder. "Judges don't like to see a bye win, so you've got to do something really spectacular—find a couple birds on the back course."

Sandy smiled. "Hey, aren't you the one who said, 'Who cares about winning? We're here just to have a good time'?"

"Yea, but this is the Windsor crowd against . . . Who are we again? *Fox Pass?*"

Jimmy knelt on one knee as he spoke to Sandy's Brittany. "I counted five birds that flew onto the back course. Think you can find one or two, Annie?" The Brit smiled her open-mouthed dog's smile back at Jimmy, and he turned and announced, "She says, 'It's a piece of cake.'"

"How are you fixed for shells?"

Sandy dug into his jacket pocket and brought out just a pair of green paper cases.

"Two!" George took a double handful of 16-gauge shells from his own coat and and put them in Sandy's pocket. "Here. These aren't doing me any good now. But remember what my grandfather used to say: *'Donna you miss the fezz.'*"

Sandy worked the action of his old 97, chambering a shell. He grinned at John. "You told me this was going to be fun."

"It would be a lot of fun to beat Brownie's crowd," John said wistfully. "Find a few birds first, *then* have fun."

George waved a finger in his face as he started off: "And *donna miss!*"

At the breakaway Sonny looked at the Brittany and asked, "Without a tail, how do you know if she's pointing?"

Tom answered before Sandy could. "You won't have any problem. These Brittanies are supposed to be the coming thing. I remember reading something about them. They used to be poachers' dogs in France." After a moment he added, "And if that ain't the definition of a meat dog, I don't know what is."

When she was waved ahead, Annie cast to the left into the woods instead of straight ahead. Sandy whistled for her. When she didn't return, he left the path and went into the brush himself. Tom went with him.

The Brit was standing on a set of pheasant tracks in the snow, pointing into a barberry thicket. The pheasant got up before Sandy was in position, and, unsure of where the judge was, he hesitated until he heard Tom behind him saying, *"Shoot, dammit!"* The bird tumbled at the sound of his gun, and Annie brought it in.

They came out of the woods into an open field that was the back course. The weight of the pheasant in his game pocket did little to ease the tension he felt. Sandy knew he was supposed to be enjoying this, but he felt not only the scrutiny of the judges but also the critical eyes of the several watchers who trailed along behind in entourage fashion. In the snow the footprints of the other hunters who had passed earlier showed they all had followed an old cart road along the wooded edge. Sandy tried to picture where a pheasant that had been flushed and missed in the bird field would have flown. He whistled to his dog and angled across the field, making new tracks in the snow as he went.

The Brit crossed a low stone fence and cast ahead on the far side. Suddenly she turned and pointed back at the wall. A pheasant ran out from between the rocks, saw the men, and sprung into the air. Sandy waited, then, when the bird was at the top of its climb, he centered the rooster. Annie was there when the bird hit the ground, and brought it proudly in to Sandy.

"I'll carry that for you—you don't want to get weighted down." Tom winked as he spoke. He turned to Sonny, "Any questions about how a Brittany points without benefit of a tail?"

"No." The other judge shook his head. "But shouldn't the dog wait to be told to retrieve?"

Tom laughed. "Sure. But this, Sonny, is a real meat dog." He motioned to Sandy. "Go ahead on up to the bird field."

Minutes later, as they were crossing back toward the cart road, the Brit caught scent and began working toward a cattail swamp below the field. Sandy turned to Tom. "She's got a runner. I'd like to follow her."

"I'll kick you in the pants if you don't."

Just a few scattered patches of snow remained in this end of the field, but here and there the tracks of a pheasant were intermingled with the Brittany's. The field ended abruptly at a beaver pond, with the swamp stretching away beyond. The dog stopped, pointing into a seemingly barren patch of snow.

"She's got him pinned." Having said it, now Sandy tried to believe it himself. Tentatively he approached the point. The rooster that had somehow hidden himself in the sparse grass jumped into the afternoon sky. The shot was an easy one, but the bird took a pair of hits before falling, just as Sandy was about to fire for the third time.

The pheasant lay across the pond in plain sight, but Annie veered into the cattails when she was sent after it. Sandy whistled and waved her to the left, but she paused only long enough to glance back at him. He recognized the signs and quickly searched into his pockets for more of George's shells.

His Brit could be heard breaking through thin ice in the swamp, then yet another pheasant clattered into the air in an extravaganza of color and noise. Sonny had exaggerated about the size of the rooster, but not by much: The bird had in-curved spurs and a half-inch of fringe on his yard-long tail feathers, but later, the part Sandy remembered most clearly was the way the bird's wings struck the head of a cattail during the moment it sprung from the frozen swamp, and the small cloud of fluff that floated on the breeze afterward. That, and the unforgettable image of Annie coming out of the weeds into the December sunshine with the copper-breasted bird held high.

As SANDY CAME into the bird field with the judges close behind him carrying the four pheasants, the scene could have been out of one of Rudyard Kipling's stories. Annie hunted through the maze of old scent in the field to find the one bird that had been planted just for her. Sandy lifted his cap and approached her point. His phantoms of tension had vanished, and he grinned as he recalled John's parting words: He was now going to have some fun.

The bird flushed and crossed the field, gaining the altitude needed to clear the tall maples beyond. The moment passed when he ordinarily would have taken the bird, and the cross shot became a quartering shot and then a very long going-away shot when Sandy finally put the 97 to his shoulder and fired. There was a long instant when he was sure he'd missed, and he regretted showing off on this last bird . . . but then the shot string caught the pheasant and it fell through the bare branches, tumbling to finally land beyond the wall at the edge of the field.

George and Jimmy and John came out into the bird field to shake Sandy's hand. Amid the laughter, brags, and praise Annie delivered the final pheasant of the day to her master. After Sandy took the bird from her, he lifted his dog in his arms. "You're a good girl, Annie."

"*I guess she is.*" John scratched the Brit's ears.

"Look at that." Jimmy pointed to the parking lot, where the three vehicles of the Windsor crowd were just pulling out.

George laughed. "I guess they're not going to stick around to find out who took second and third."

Sandy put his dog back on the ground, and they all started back toward the clubhouse. "So what do you think of this pointin' spaniel, judge?"

"My hat's off to her," said Sonny. "Tom's right—she's a real meat dog."

"Meat dog, hell," Tom said. "That is one mighty fine *bird* dog."

Of Ringers and Leaners

ROBERT LEANED against the porch railing, watching the progress on the skeet field immediately in front of the clubhouse. Five men were engaged in what was supposed to be a game, but when one of them missed a high house shot from station three, the silence was louder than any sarcastic laughter could ever be. He shook his head, smiling to himself. Inside the clubhouse his father made conversation with some fellows who were waiting for someone else. Robert wondered if there existed a man *anywhere* with whom his father couldn't make small talk. He glanced at his watch: It had been twenty minutes they had been waiting to shoot. He went to the window inside.

"Mind if we go out ourselves? Field three is open."

The fellow in charge of registrations was on the phone, but he looked up at Robert's request. "Sure, go ahead. You'll have to push your own buttons, though—all my trap boys are tied up right now."

Robert nodded. Actually he preferred it that way. There were several groups of fellows at the club he enjoyed teaming with to fill out a five-man squad, but most were like those he had been watching on the porch: They took their fun much too seriously. He and his father walked down the hill to field three. Behind them the sounds of shotguns repeated a staccato cadence.

The remnants of thousands of empty shells littered the field, and just beyond the shooting area the ground seemed to blush fluorescent orange among the weeds, almost as if some exotic wildflower blossomed there rather than a six-inch layer of broken skeet. They walked to station one at the far end of the field. Robert leaned his gun against the high house building and took up the electrical push-button device that set off the traps.

"Go ahead, Dad. I'll shoot after you."

His father stood on the square concrete pad that marked the shooter's position, flexing his arm and shouldering his gun in preparation. When he seemed ready, he asked, "High house first?"

Robert nodded.

"Okay . . . *Pull!*"

The target flew out immediately above his father's head. Robert waited, but no shot was fired. His father said, "Oh, *high* house first. Go ahead, let me have another one . . . *Pull!*"

Another target flew out, this one shot at and missed.

"Take another try, Dad."

"High house again?"

"Yes. Same shot."

A third target flew, but after his father's shot it, too, landed unbroken with the previous two.

"What am I doing wrong, Bob?"

"I don't think you held under it."

"Yeah." His father nodded to himself. "Why didn't you remind me?"

Robert smiled a thin smile but said nothing. He wasn't given to handing out advice to the man who had taught him to shoot. "Go ahead, low house now," Robert said. The target was called for, and his father tracked it until it floated just above his left shoulder before pulverizing it. "That's the way," Robert said. He remembered a younger time when this now-old man had been a good shot—a time when everything his father did seemed miraculous and larger than life. That same young man still lived inside his father, a younger man who could shoot well and took pride in his shooting. A younger man, too, who knew nothing of things like cataracts and angina. Lately, enjoying his father's company took more patience than serious skeet shooters were willing to spend. Robert was glad they had the field to themselves.

At station two his father shot late and broke the high house target when it was on its way down, twenty yards or so beyond the stake. He turned to Robert. "Did I hit that?"

"Right between the feathers."

"Better send the dog to fetch him in," his father joked, and turned back to the station.

"I'm afraid she'll bump up those other three that landed over there just a moment ago," he replied. They both laughed.

Before Robert could take his turn at the second station, a pair of men came down the hill from the clubhouse. They carried shotguns. "Mind if we jump in?"

"Of course not," his father was quick to answer. "Go ahead and shoot station one—we'll wait for you."

Robert nodded a terse greeting to the pair. One was someone he knew only as Marty, a regular shooter at the club. The other man wore a green baseball cap. Robert didn't know him, but if he was a friend of loud-mouthed Marty, he couldn't have much in the way of judgment, he thought. As a longtime member of the club, Marty had a way of looking down his nose at "nonregulars" like Robert who didn't shoot every weekend. A definitive character trait of Marty's, evident to anyone who shot just one round with him, was that the man never missed a target as the result of poor shooting: It was always a bum reload or the trap boy's pull or the wind or his new jacket or the Coriolis effect—*anything* but his own fault. Robert handed the push-buttons to the fellow in the green cap.

Both men shot with the mechanical precision of practiced skeet shooters, centering each target over the twenty-three–yard stake. They finished quickly and came up behind Robert and his father at station two.

"Hi there," said Marty. "Thanks for waiting. We've shot together before, haven't we?" He spoke to Robert.

"Sure, a few times." He hesitated, then decided not to introduce his father. Instead he took his position and called for his targets.

When Robert finished, Marty said to him, "Now I remember you: You're the one that uses that screwy international style." He referred to Robert's refusal to follow modern skeet dictum and shoulder the gun before calling for the target. There were any number of people who could have told Robert his shooting style was screwy without making him grit his teeth. Marty wasn't one of them.

At station three Robert's father missed both targets.

"That low house needs a good three and a half feet of lead," advised Marty.

Amenable as always, his father listened attentively. *Three and a half feet.* Marty broke targets. There were no two ways about it, he was accomplished at the mechanics of skeet shooting. But as such he fancied himself an expert shot, charged with the duty of instructing those less fortunate who missed once in a while—even if the errant shooter had been tracking cross shots for fifty years or so. Three and a half feet. Robert smiled to himself but found no humor in the situation. Instead he looked into the sky, searching his memory for a glimpse of something silver spinning in the air.

At station four Robert missed his first target of the round. He steeled himself for the inevitable gem of advice from Marty, but his father had engaged the other two men in conversation and was relating a story about fishing in Maine. His miss went unnoticed. Robert smiled.

Marty missed one of the cross shots at station four, also. It was his first miss. "I took a chip out of that, didn't I?" It was more a statement than a question.

"The hell you did!" replied Green Baseball Cap. They evidently had a beer bet going. Maybe he's got Marty's number after all, thought Robert.

His father got some more expert advice at station five, with Marty pointing out the flight path of the targets as if it were some form of erudition only he possessed. When his father missed the low house bird, Marty shook his head but said nothing. Robert looked up once again but still couldn't find in his memory the metal object he was searching for. Gerard Ford still carried it around with him, so he really had no reason to expect it would appear just because he was looking for it. He stepped close to Marty and looked away as he spoke, not wanting his father to hear.

"We'll be okay, Marty—really. We're not out here to learn anything important, just to shoot a couple of rounds and sniff some Red Dot. It doesn't mean doodlysquat whether or not . . ."

"Oh, I know." Marty cut him off. "I just hate to see someone make the same obvious mistakes over and over."

Robert took a breath as if to reply, then thought better of it and took his place on the shooting pad. I should have offered to punch his lights out, he told himself. At times he became impatient with himself for putting up with situations where he was expected to be polite to fools. Before he called for his targets, he paused a moment, listening to his own thoughts. The sky in his memory remained empty. He imagined that by now he would have heard it strike the ground some-where behind him—a Zippo lighter would make quite a clink when it hit the concrete after falling from so high up.

When Green Baseball Cap took his turn at five, he only nicked the low house target.

"*Ha!*" Marty nearly shouted. "*We're even.*"

"He took a piece out of it." Robert's voice was flat.

"Yeah, I thought I did, too," said Green Baseball Cap.

Robert glanced at Marty out of the corner of his eye. He looked genuinely disappointed.

"Hell, blind as even I am, I could see that he dusted that one," his father said. "That's another one you'll have to send the dog for, Bob." They all grinned. Except Marty.

They moved to the pad at station six. From the pad Robert's father looked back at him. "High house first?"

Robert nodded.

In turn, each target was broken cleanly. His father gave a thumbs-up sign as he left the pad. "Not bad for an old fart, huh?"

"Doubles now, Mister Cody," Robert said.

"Oh, yeah. I forgot." His father stepped back onto the shooting station, then glanced over his shoulder at Robert. "And watch that 'Mister Cody' stuff. On his best day, Buffalo Bill *wished* he could shoot like me."

When the pair of targets flew, both were missed.

Marty nearly spat in disgust. "You shot at the *high house first!*"

Robert closed his eyes. Now he could see it. Of course, his perspective was a lot closer to the ground back those thirty-five years, and the two familiar men in canvas shooting coats appeared much younger than today, but the blue October sky and the edge of the cornfield hadn't changed. Neither had the single tail feather Gerard waved at his father. "I think most of that pheasant was just in front of this, Hank. Ha ha." Across the years he could still hear Gerard's deep voice and slow laugh. "If this was horse shoes, I'd have to give you a point for a leaner on that bird. Ha ha." The constant kidding that had always gone on between the two gentle men could never be mistaken for anything else, not even by a little boy of six. Maybe the incident would never have happened if Robert hadn't been there to have seen his father miss, but his father grinned and said, "Go ahead, throw your hat in the air—I'll show you the difference between a ringer and a leaner." Gerard had replied, "Hell, I'll do better than that . . ." and had tossed his cigarette lighter high overhead. Five shots later Gerard walked into the weeds at the edge of the field and retrieved his much-battered but still workable Zippo. But across the years the memory of it dancing against the blue azimuth of the cloudless sky, falling only to rocket upward again with each successive shot, tumbling over and over in the sunlight, stayed with him. And so had the pride that a little boy felt for his father at that moment in time.

They continued. His father, inexplicably, broke the last six targets, including both of the tough overhead shots at station eight. He nudged Robert as they waited. "Hey, I think I've got the ol' eye back. Watch me smoke 'em on this next round." The young man inside his father smiled out at Robert.

Green Baseball Cap was the last to shoot, but on his final low house option he lifted his head and missed cleanly.

"*Ha!*" said Marty. "We're even again." He grinned and drew out a pack of cigarettes. "And I *still* think you dropped low five, too," he added.

Robert could think of several charitable things he might say to a friend who had just blown a perfect round on the last shot, but instead he stepped closer to Marty. "Say, that's a really nice-looking lighter you've got there, Marty. Mind if I look at it for a minute?"

Brown Feathers from My Game Vest

THE STATIC on my radio stops, and overhead I hear the scrape of a chair being pushed back, then footsteps. The cellar door is opened, and a moment later my nylon-faced hunting pants land in a heap at the bottom of the stairs.

"Steven?"

"Hello." I put down the whittling knife and shake the wood shavings from my lap.

"Your cuffs are fixed. And I found a tear in the seat, too. What else have you got?"

"My vest has some rips in it. I'll bring it up."

"Why don't you get yourself a new one? I've been patching that old thing for years."

"Bean's wants forty bucks for them now. I'll put it on my Christmas list."

There is a telling pause on the stair landing, then, "You might as well bring it up."

I look through the rack of my hunting clothes for anything else in need of mending before being forgotten for another year. There is a wool shirt with a torn elbow as well as my old poplin vest.

Some final instructions come down the stairs: "Make sure you clean out the pockets. I don't want sticks and dirt all over my sewing room."

"Okay, Maggie."

After a pause, she asks, "Who's Maggie?"

"Jiggs's wife."

"*Insect!*" The door closes.

Not bad. She's not usually that quick.

The buffalo plaid shirt has only a dried leaf in its buttoned pocket—one I had intended to look up but forgot. I stand at the trash bucket and turn out the vest pockets. During the course of the hunting season they collect enough twigs to start a good-sized barbecue. I unzip the gamebag and turn it inside out . . .

Suddenly a pair of woodcock are in the air, twisting up through the near-leafless aspens above Hazel's point. I track the higher bird to the top of his climb, and he folds at my shot, falling back into the branches. His fall dislodges a single golden aspen leaf which flutters to the ground as I stand listening to the echoes of my shot . . .

Two blacks ease over the treetops and into the shadow cast by the rising sun. Win and I crouch together, watching intently as they bank around the rig. After one has fallen among the decoys and Win is on her way to the bird, I notice a float of feathers hanging in the air like a three-dimensional punctuation mark on the spot where duck and shot came together . . .

A pheasant climbs into the overcast sky from the last corner of the asparagus bed. Feathers fly at both of my shots, but the cock glides off on set wings. I send Hazel after him, and she is gone for an uncomfortably long five minutes. Standing on the farm road and peering into the riverside tangles, I happen to glance to my left in time to see her emerge from the thicket two hundred yards away. The burden she carries causes her to hold her head awkwardly, but her tail is high and she fairly prances to me and delivers a bird I have no right to have expected her to find . . .

I stand in the clearing by the cedar I had singled out as my marker when the bird fell. All of my hope is out in the laurel thickets with Win, and I follow her progress with my ears. When her bell stops, I whistle to her, and she trots through the under-brush and vaults over the stone wall into the clearing. In her mouth she carries the cock grouse I wasn't sure I had hit. His tail is spread as she carries him. After I have taken the bird and thanked her, she sits at my feet. A single fluffy breast feather remains clinging to the moisture on her nose . . .

I look to where my two bird dogs lie sleeping on their cellar rugs and bid them both a silent thanks. Then I reach into the trash bucket to find which of the brown feathers from my game vest fits which memory.

Acknowledgments

There are any number of people who deserve thanks for their help in making this book pass from a dream into a reality. Chief among them:

Mark Dilts, whose name appears on the dedication page and who had the courage long ago to criticize a novice's efforts and shepherd him through his early years.

Jay Cassell, who wrote the foreword and has gently demanded only my best.

Susan Mulak, my wife, critic, and ever my greatest fan.

But at the same time there is another group of people who helped me along, and whom I must thank with equal fervor. In no particular order they are *Hal Borland, Burton Spiller, Thomas McIntyre, Gene Hill, Ed Zern, Robert Ruark, Havilah Babcock, Charles Waterman, Joel Vance, Corey Ford, Patrick McManus, Bob Brister,* and *Vance Bourjaily.* Although I have never exchanged a spoken word with any of these men, they have often stood at my shoulder as I worked, shaking their heads and advising me through their example that there is no "outdoor writing," only "good writing" and then, just "everything else."

Thank you all.

Postscript

The lady I was with closed the magazine and laid it aside on an empty chair, and there was a pause before she spoke. "How do you do it? Not write—I know what kind of hard work is involved in that. But your stuff all seems to have a presence to it—little details, descriptions of how a plant looked or a bird sounded—things that bring people into your stories. You obviously do it on purpose—but how?"

As is my wont when I am at a loss for words, I made a small joke. Her compliment pleased me each time I thought of it for days afterward, but at that moment I had no answer for her.

It was May, and we were on the river going shad fishing. Dad's eyes had gotten so bad he needed someone along with him to knot his lures onto the monofilament. I was tying the darts onto the lines while he was at the wheel of the boat, heading up to where the 391 bridge crossed.

"Hey," he turned to holler above the drone of the motor. "Do you smell those grape blossoms?"

I lifted my nose in an imitation of a cartoon character smelling an apple pie someone has rested on a distant window ledge. I sniffed deeply and smelt something more faint than fragrant, nodded to him, and went back to tying blood knots.

It took a while, but slowly I realized that in that moment I had found the answer to the elusive question the lady had asked me years before.

Credits for the epigrams